Thank You For Holding.

Your Injury Is Important to Us

———

A Lightheartedly Serious Look

At Workers' Compensation Reform

Robert H. Wilson

WorkCompCollege.com Press

Lakewood Ranch, Florida - 2026

Thank You For Holding.

[ISBN: 979-8-234-02613-2]

First Edition

Printed in the United States of America

www.WorkCompCollege.com
www.bobsclutteredesk.com

For the 7,000 who are injured at work today, and every day, and for those who fight to make the system worthy of them.

"Although the world is full of suffering, it is also full of the overcoming of it."

— Helen Keller

"The only thing that saves us from the bureaucracy is its inefficiency."

— Eugene McCarthy

Contents

Part II: A Better Way Forward

Foreword

The first time I heard Bob Wilson talk was at the Tennessee workers' compensation education conference over a decade ago. He was the keynote speaker, and I was the relatively new administrator of Tennessee Bureau of Workers' Compensation and also the person being held responsible for a favorable outcome to the newly implemented reform of Tennessee's workers' compensation system.

He was funny and in the beginning of his talk I thought he had a calling as a stand-up comedian. Then he challenged the workers' compensation world to embrace the concept of "workers' recovery." It was apparent that his true calling was to improve workers' compensation.

Bob presented real life cases to demonstrate the difference that the "workers' recovery" approach could make. The more he talked, the more convinced I was that he had put his finger on what was needed to fulfill the promise of workers' compensation which was the goal of the Tennessee bureau.

In the years that followed Bob used the bully pulpit at WorkersCompensation.com and then WorkCompCollege.com, to preach the gospel of treating injured workers like valuable people who need assistance to regain their pre-injury life back, not just a claim number. In Tennessee we embraced Bob's view and became an advocate of focusing on helping employees recover from day one which we believe was in the best interests of both injured workers and their employers. As the years have gone by, more and more employers in our state have adopted this approach with good results.

With the publication of this book, you will receive humorous reference (this is not an oxymoron) on "Workers' Recovery." You can have his insights and his humor at any time with ***Thank you for Holding; Your Injury is Important to Us.*** The title tells you an important aspect of this book. Bob's characteristic "no holds barred" approach is there throughout. Reading this book is like having Bob in the room with you. The heart of the book is a breakdown on the points of the "Workers' Recovery" approach that Bob has shared through the years with the humor to soften the points that may make us wince.

If you are a Bob Wilson fan you will greatly enjoy this book. If you haven't heard his message, you will enjoy his sense of humor and his sharp insights into both the problems of "workers' compensation" and the promise of Employee's Recovery will be enlightening. They jump off every page.

Beneath his pithy insights into the problems of current practices are his views on what can be better. His prescriptions can lead to a system that responds more rapidly, more humanly, and more efficiently at helping injured workers recover and return to a life worth living. Interestingly, these prescriptions can also lead to improved satisfaction among employers and even lower costs at the end of the day.

Today's workers' compensation system is a vast improvement for employees over the "common law" environment at the beginning of the twentieth century. Then it was almost impossible for workers to get any restitution for losses caused by work related injuries. The "Grand Compromise" of workers' compensation was a great step toward an approach that struck an appropriate balance between the interests of employees and employers. As the decades rolled by and incremental changes were made due to new laws, efficiency measures, and an increasing number of interest groups with vested interests in the system we have lost our focus on the linchpin of an improved system – the employee. ***Thank you for Holding. Your Injury is Important to Us*** can get us on the right track.

Abbie Hudgens, MPA, ARM, AIC

Preface
Over a Decade in the Making

I can honestly say that this book has been well over a decade in the making. It was in 2012 when the concept of rebranding workers' compensation first came to me. It was 2013 when I first presented "Workers' Recovery" in my blog, From Bob's Cluttered Desk. Since that time, it has evolved and taken shape, with critical missing details slowly developing, filling in the gaps. There have been numerous articles promoting the idea, and I have endeavored to at least mention the concept in over 200 conference presentations. It has, without exception, received excellent response every time.

It has even served in the foundation of WorkCompCollege.com, which I co-founded with Mark Pew and Donald Abrams in 2022. The college's flagship Workers' Recovery Professional Certification program mirrors the ideology and positions reflected in this book. As a testament to the strength of the Workers' Recovery concept, many workers' comp professionals from all industry sectors came forth to help us establish the program, formalizing the concept through training and education.

Yet the true genesis of this book can be traced to an exercise in which I was given the honor of participating in 2015. The editor of the IAIABC Journal proposed a project; a project that would help coalesce a collection of loosely connected dots and ultimately provide the foundation for the pages now before you.

Robert Aurbach, the editor I mentioned, asked me if I would be interested in writing an article for the International Association of Industrial Accident Boards and Commission's quarterly publication, The Journal. He wanted me to write a piece called "The Case for Workers' Recovery." As the concept evolved, Aurbach made a unique proposition. He suggested I write my article supporting the concept of Workers' Recovery, while he had invited another person to opine on their vision of what the future of workers' comp should be. We would then each write a critique of the other's article, and all four pieces would be published as a "point – counter point" style debate. I thought it was a great idea and immediately accepted. It was only after accepting I asked a critical question. A question I should have asked before. Who is the other author?

Aurbach's answer was straight and matter of fact. John Burton.

Shit.

Dr. John F. Burton, Jr. is Professor Emeritus and former Dean in the School of Management and Labor Relations at Rutgers University and Professor Emeritus in the School of Industrial and Labor Relations at Cornell University. He has a law degree and a Ph.D. in Economics from the University of Michigan. He is, according to the National Academy of Social Insurance, "one of the nation's foremost scholars on workers' compensation." Burton is best known in our industry as the chairman of the National Commission on State Workmen's Compensation Laws, having been appointed to the post by President Nixon in 1972.

By contrast, I was a website developer, businessperson, and at that point a 4-year Cluttered Desk blogger. I didn't parachute into comp; I had come into the industry sideways through the trenches — from restaurant and hospitality management, where I first learned about workers' comp the hard way (a story I'll share later in this book), to human resources and technical recruiting, then through running WorkersCompensation.com, where I spent years interacting with millions of visitors including the injured workers the system was supposed to serve. I have a bachelor's degree in business administration from Fort Lewis College in Durango, Colorado. And regarding that college experience, I wasn't exactly a standout student. While some people graduate Summa or Magna Cum Laude, my graduation was more along the lines of "Thank You Dear Laude."

And now I had somehow gotten into the position of publicly debating one of the most respected minds of the industry. Yikes.

In reality, it was a great experience. I wrote "The Case for Workers' Recovery." Dr. Burton wrote, "Should There Be a 21st Century National Commission on State Workers' Compensation Laws?" I critiqued his article with the response titled, "Four Possible Rights Can Still Make a Potential Wrong," while his response to mine was simply titled, "Some Observations by John Burton on 'The Case for Workers' Recovery' by Robert Wilson."

At the time, it was a nerve-wracking endeavor, as I did not see Burton's response to my article until they were all published. For four months I could only envision the public thrashing I was about to endure. But in the end, while we definitely have different ideas about where workers' compensation should go, Dr. Burton was very kind to me in his response. The entire exercise turned out to be a successful and worthwhile enterprise.

The best part about the entire thing is that it forced me at the time to coalesce the concept from a loosely defined suggestion into a more thoughtful, detailed proposal. "The Case for Workers' Recovery" took a simple ethereal idea and gave it structure and definition. The soul of an idea gained a more clearly defined body in this exercise.

And it is that article series that has served as the foundation for this book. Much of the content comes from it, and numerous blog articles that followed. I want to thank Robert Aurbach within these pages, for they may not exist in this form if not for his early support and innovative idea.

As you will soon read, Workers' Recovery is not a call for revolution, it is a proposal for evolution. A much-needed change for a more than one hundred-year-old industry facing unprecedented changes in economics, technology, and societal expectations. The clock is ticking.

Let's get started. Time, like many injured workers caught in an antiquated and outdated system, is a wastin'.

Chapter 1
Welcome to the System

The moment you get hurt at work, a clock starts ticking. Not the kind that counts the minutes until your shift ends. This one counts the minutes until a system you never knew existed potentially swallows you whole.

In many cases, nobody hands you a brochure. Nobody sits you down and says, "Let me walk you through what happens next." Instead, someone shoves a clipboard at you, probably while you're still wondering why your back just made a sound like a knuckle cracking in a library. The clipboard has forms. The forms have questions. The questions assume you know things you absolutely do not know. And somewhere, in an office you've never seen, a file has just been opened with your name on it. But in most cases, you won't be a name. You'll be a number.

Welcome to the system.

* * *

Workers' compensation is one of America's greatest social achievements. It really is. It was born from the "Grand Bargain," as it is commonly called, or the "Great Compromise," as it is referred to in some circles, over a century ago. At the time it was a brilliantly simple idea: if you get hurt on the job, your employer covers your medical care and a portion of your wages while you recover. In exchange, you give up the right to sue. Employer gets predictability. Worker gets security. Everybody shakes hands and moves on.

That was the idea, anyway.

There will be points while consuming the content of this tome that workers' comp professionals may think it is criticizing *them.* It might feel at points extremely personal. That will be an unfortunate and inaccurate interpretation. In reality, any criticisms in this book are directed at the *system*, rather than the people that toil within it. There are many wonderful, well-meaning people in workers' compensation, doing what they can in a system that has gradually evolved into an overly complex and heavily regulated environment. Similarly, not all industry players will necessarily reflect some of the more negative observations here, as some currently embrace and deploy the positive recommendations contained within this book. No, this work is focused on the system itself, and addresses the weaknesses and faults developed over more than 100 years of procedural evolution.

And what it has become, over the course of a hundred-plus years of legislative tinkering, jurisdictional variation, lobbying, cost-cutting, and bureaucratic expansion, is something considerably less elegant than that originally envisioned. What started as a handshake has become a Rube Goldberg machine — an enormously complex apparatus with thousands of moving parts, competing interests, and enough paperwork to deforest a small nation. It competently manages the newly reported injuries and occupational illnesses of more than 7,000 Americans each and every day. That's the good news. The less good news is that "competently manages" and "actually helps people get better" are not always the same thing.

And that distinction is what this book is about.

* * *

What's in a Name? (More Than You Think)

Let's start with something that seems trivially simple, but is in fact profoundly important: the name.

Workers' Compensation.

Say it out loud. What does it promise? Compensation. Money. Remuneration. It's right there in the title. And that's exactly what most injured workers, blissfully ignorant of the system that now controls their life, hear when they enter the system. It's the first signal the system sends, and it's the wrong one.

I spent years running WorkersCompensation.com, a site that during my tenure served millions of visitors annually. Without fail, when an injured worker new to the system reached out — either through direct contact or our discussion forums — their question, tucked in alongside the long and detailed description of their injury, was almost always the same: "How much will I be paid?" Or "How much will I make?" Or, more unsettlingly, "How big will my settlement be?" Not "How do I get better?" Not "How long until I'm back to normal?" Not "How do I make sure I get adequate care?" The question is always about money. Always.

And I don't blame them for a second. The system told them that's what this is about. It's in the name.

Words mean things. This isn't motivational-poster philosophy; it's science. Research has demonstrated that a single word can influence the expression of genes that regulate physical and emotional stress. Studies have shown that simply modifying the phrasing of pain-related questions to patients produces wide variation in reported pain levels. You can literally change how much something hurts by changing how you ask about it. If words can do that, imagine what an entire system built around the wrong word is doing.

That's why I've been arguing, for years now, that workers' compensation needs a new name. It should be called **Workers' Recovery**.

Not because a name change is a magic wand. But because "recovery" sets an expectation that everyone — including the least educated injured worker entering the system for the first time — can understand. And it is a continual reminder for those charged with their care. Recovery means getting better. It means healing. It means returning to a life worth living. "Compensation" just means getting paid. And if getting paid is the goal, then the system is, however unintentionally, building a pipeline to dependency rather than a pathway to healing.

* * *

Your First Day in the Machine

But we're getting ahead of ourselves. Before we can fix the system, we need to understand what it feels like to be inside it. So let's walk through what happens when you get hurt at work. Not what's supposed to happen in theory. What actually happens.

You're at work. Something goes wrong. Maybe you slip, maybe you lift something the wrong way, maybe a piece of equipment has other ideas about your continued physical integrity. Whatever happens, you're hurt. And your first thought, before anything about forms or claims or compensation, is probably something along the lines of a word your mother told you not to say.

Your second thought is to tell somebody. This is where things start to get interesting, and by "interesting" I mean "profoundly annoying." Your supervisor's reaction may range from genuine concern to mild inconvenience to barely concealed suspicion that you're making the whole thing up. The good ones ask if you're okay. The mediocre ones ask if you can finish your shift. The bad ones ask if anyone saw it happen.

Then the paperwork begins. Oh, the paperwork. If you've ever done your taxes, bought a house, or applied for a government security clearance, you have some frame of reference for what's coming. If you've done all three simultaneously while someone periodically asks you to describe "the mechanism of injury" in clinical terminology, you're getting closer.

You have to deal with the First Report of Injury, the claim form, the employer's report, the authorization for medical treatment, the selection of a treating physician, which in some states you get to choose and in others is chosen for you. And in some states, you can change doctors. In others you can't. Unless the good doctor dies. Even then there are technicalities that could strap your care to the dearly departed Doc. Regardless, each form asks for information you've already provided on the previous form, as if the system is testing whether your story stays consistent, like a detective in a procedural drama who keeps asking you where you were on the night of the injury.

And you haven't even seen a doctor yet, dead or alive.

* * *

A System That Works (Just Not Well Enough)

Here's the thing — and I want to be fair about this, because fairness matters when you're about to spend an entire book poking holes in something. Workers' compensation works. It has worked for over a century. The Grand Bargain was a genuine achievement, and the system that grew from it has served this country through world wars, economic booms and busts, technological revolutions, and a complete transformation of what "work" even means. It's not broken in the sense that it needs to be demolished and rebuilt from scratch.

It's broken in the sense that your car is broken when the engine runs fine but the steering pulls hard to the left, the air conditioning only works in winter, and the GPS keeps trying to drive you into a lake. The fundamental machinery is sound. The direction it's heading is the problem.

And where is it heading? Toward a world where the system manages claims rather than people. Where "success" is measured in cost containment rather than lives restored. Where the word "compensation" has become so thoroughly embedded in the DNA of the enterprise that everyone — employers, insurers, legislators, and the injured workers themselves — has internalized the idea that this is fundamentally about money, not about getting better.

Meanwhile, the challenges facing the system are getting bigger, not smaller. We're dealing with an aging workforce, a growing obesity epidemic, increasing rates of chronic conditions like diabetes, and a cultural shift toward what some researchers call the "disability mindset" — a growing acceptance, even expectation, of dependency on benefits. Despite dramatic declines in injury rates and major advances in medical care and technology over the past two decades, we're seeing unprecedented increases in injury duration, days away from work, and people being placed on permanent disability status.

Let me put that more plainly: we're getting better at preventing injuries and treating them, and yet people are taking longer to recover and more of them are ending up permanently disabled. If that doesn't tell you there's something wrong with the system itself, I'm not sure what would.

* * *

The Person Behind the Claim Number

A number of years ago, at a meeting of the IAIABC — that's the International Association of Industrial Accident Boards and Commissions, which can actually be more fun than it sounds — a representative of an insurance carrier, lamenting the excessive regulation multi-state entities must navigate, said something that stopped the room cold. She said that she sometimes felt "the claimant is no longer relevant to the process."

It is a truly sad statement, but not the saddest part. Not a single person in the room disagreed.

Think about that. A system designed to help injured workers, and the professionals inside it acknowledge that the injured worker has become almost incidental to the machine that's supposed to serve them. We've built a system so complex, so layered with regulations and procedures and competing interests, that the human being at the center of it has become an afterthought. An input variable. A claim number.

Every one of those claim numbers is a person who wants to pick up their child without wincing. A person who wants to walk the dog again. A person who wants to bend down and smell the roses — literally, not metaphorically. Every one of them woke up that morning thinking it was just another day at work, and by the end of it, their life had changed in ways they didn't see coming and don't fully understand.

They deserve better than a system that puts them on hold.

* * *

What This Book Is (And What It Isn't)

This book is a case for doing things differently. Not for burning the house down, but for renovating it — aggressively, and with a much better floor plan.

I'm going to take you on a tour of the workers' compensation system as it exists today. We'll follow an injured worker from the moment of injury through the paperwork avalanche, the employer shuffle, the insurance labyrinth, the medical merry-go-round, and the often-clumsy return to work. Along the way, I'm going to make fun of things. Quite a lot of things, actually. Because humor is a powerful weapon, and I've found it's extremely useful when deployed in balance. Sometimes the most effective way to expose a problem is to make people laugh at the absurdity of it.

But this isn't just a comedy routine. Behind the jokes, there's a serious argument: that workers' compensation — Workers' Recovery, as I believe it should be known — can and must evolve. It must be refocused toward different priorities. It must streamline procedures and produce better medical outcomes. Communication between all stakeholders, especially employers and employees, must be dramatically improved. Better expectations must be established. And above all, it must place priority on results rather than process.

Workers' Recovery is not a repudiation of workers' compensation. Think of it as workers' compensation version 2.0, with the same foundational principles, the same Grand Bargain, or Great Compromise, but upgraded for the 21st century, with the focus placed squarely where it belongs: on helping injured workers get better and get back to living.

We owe it to the 7,000 people who will get hurt at work today. And the 7,000 who will get hurt tomorrow. And the day after that.

So thank you for holding. Your injury is important to us. And by the end of this book, I hope you'll agree that we can do a whole lot better than putting people on hold.

Chapter 2
The Injury: It's Not Just a Scratch

In Monty Python and the Holy Grail, King Arthur and his knights encounter a cave guarded by what appears to be an ordinary rabbit. "It's just a little bunny rabbit!" scoffs one of the knights, moments before the beast launches itself at the company and begins removing heads with the efficiency of a corporate restructuring. The knights, having thoroughly underestimated the threat, are forced into a panicked retreat, leaving behind several colleagues who will no longer be needing their armor.

"Run away! Run away!"

If you've ever reported a workplace injury, this scene may feel uncomfortably familiar. Not the part about the killer rabbit, necessarily. The part about the minimizing. The part where everyone around you looks at what happened and says, essentially, "It's just a little bunny rabbit."

* * *

The Minimizing Machine

There is a powerful gravitational force within the workers' compensation universe that pulls every injury toward the word "minor." It doesn't matter what actually happened. It doesn't matter how much it hurts. The system — and by "the system" I mean the entire constellation of employers, supervisors, insurers, and sometimes even the injured workers themselves — has an almost reflexive tendency to downplay, dismiss, and diminish.

The supervisor who says, "You sure you didn't just pull something?" The coworker who helpfully offers, "I had the same thing. Walked it off in a day." The HR representative who asks, "Do you really think you need to see a doctor, or can we just ice it?" The adjuster who, upon receiving the claim, mentally sorts it into the "probably nothing" pile before reading past the first paragraph.

And then there's the injured worker, who very often participates in the minimizing themselves. Because admitting you're hurt at work triggers a cascade of consequences that most people would rather avoid. There's the paperwork we discussed in Chapter 1. There's the sideways glance from the supervisor. There's the unspoken but very much felt stigma that comes with being "the person who filed a claim" and the self-criticism that if you were smarter, you wouldn't have had the accident. The "pariah" that even formerly friendly co-workers will avoid and their resentment of the extra work they must do while you are absent. So people tough it out. They work through it. They walk it off. Until they can't.

"It's just a flesh wound!" as another Monty Python character famously insisted, while missing several limbs. The system shares his optimism, if not his commitment to denial.

* * *

Not All Injuries Are Created Equal (But the Forms Are)

Workplace injuries occupy an enormous spectrum, from the minor cut that needs a bandage and a tetanus shot to the catastrophic event that changes everything. Between those extremes lies a vast middle ground of sprains, strains, fractures, repetitive motion injuries, occupational illnesses, and conditions that defy easy categorization — the kind of injuries that aren't dramatic enough for the evening news but are absolutely dramatic enough to derail a life.

The system, however, has a remarkably uniform response to all of them. Whether you've got a paper cut or a crushed vertebra, the process that kicks into gear is essentially the same. Same forms. Same reporting requirements. Same bureaucratic choreography. It's as if you walked into an emergency room with a splinter and they prepped you for surgery, or walked in with a compound fracture and they handed you an aspirin and a pamphlet.

This one-size-fits-all approach creates problems at both ends. For the genuinely minor injuries, the process itself becomes a bigger ordeal than the injury. A worker who slipped, bruised a knee, and would have been fine in three days is now filling out paperwork, visiting an approved physician, waiting for claim acceptance, and wondering whether reporting this was worth the hassle. The process doesn't just manage the injury; it becomes a secondary injury of its own.

At the other end, for the truly serious injuries, the same process that felt like overkill for a bruised knee suddenly feels woefully inadequate. The forms don't capture the terror of being told you might not walk again. The standard claims process doesn't account for the fact that your spouse hasn't slept in a week. The system treats a shattered pelvis with the same administrative machinery it uses for a sprained wrist, and then wonders why outcomes aren't better.

* * *

The Injuries You Can't See

If the system struggles with physical injuries it can see, imagine how it handles the ones it can't.

Repetitive motion injuries don't arrive with a dramatic incident report. There's no moment where a supervisor witnesses the event, no "mechanism of injury" to describe in clinical detail. Instead, there's a gradual accumulation of damage – the wrist that starts aching after years of the same motion, the shoulder that slowly loses range, the back that was fine on Monday and barely functional by Friday. Try pinpointing the "date of injury" on that. The form demands one. The body doesn't always cooperate with the form.

Occupational illnesses are even trickier. Exposure to chemicals, dust, noise, or other environmental hazards can take years or even decades to manifest as a diagnosable condition. A worker who develops a respiratory illness after twenty years of exposure faces the Kafkaesque challenge of proving that their condition is work-related when the employer they worked for in

1999 has been through three mergers, two name changes, and may no longer exist in any recognizable form. Good luck with that First Report of Injury.

And then there's the category that the system has historically been least equipped to handle: psychological injuries. The first responder who has seen things no person should have to see. The worker who develops PTSD after a workplace violence incident. The employee whose mental health has been ground down by years of hostile working conditions. These are real injuries with real consequences, and in many jurisdictions, the system either doesn't recognize them at all or treats them as a suspiciously convenient afterthought to a "real" injury.

Because if you can't see it on an X-ray, did it really happen?

* * *

What Happens When You Underestimate the Bunny

Back to our Monty Python metaphor. The knights who dismissed the Killer Rabbit paid dearly for their arrogance. They assumed the threat was small because the package was small. The workers' compensation system makes the same mistake every day.

When injuries are minimized — when an employer discourages a report, when a worker toughs it out, when an adjuster fast-tracks a claim to closure before the full picture has developed — the consequences don't disappear. They compound. The back strain that wasn't properly treated becomes a chronic condition. The worker who returned too early reinjures themselves. The psychological component that nobody addressed festers into full-blown depression, which turns a six-week claim into a six-month disability.

There's a cruel irony here. The system minimizes injuries largely in the name of cost containment. It says don't report it; it'll keep our experience mod down. Push them back to work early — it'll save on indemnity. Close the claim quickly — it'll look better on the loss run. And in the short term, those strategies do save money. In the long term, they are spectacularly, almost impressively, expensive.

And we haven't even mentioned the inherent delays that come with required approvals, investigations, initial denials, second opinions, specialist referrals, utilization review processes, prior authorization for treatments, peer review challenges to the treating physician's recommendations, formulary restrictions that delay prescribed medications, step therapy requirements that force patients to fail on cheaper treatments before approving what their doctor actually recommended, IME appointments scheduled weeks or months out, disputes between treating physicians and IME doctors over diagnosis and treatment plans, adjuster caseloads so massive that return calls take days, medical records requests sitting in queues, and — in what should be the system's most on-brand moment — injured workers who can't reach a live human being because they've been routed to an automated phone system that literally puts them on hold. Every one of these delays isn't just an administrative inconvenience. It's a clinical event. Each one stretches the gap between injury and recovery, and the research is unambiguous: the longer that gap grows, the less likely a full recovery becomes. The bunny gets a little bigger every day you pretend it isn't there.

The research is unambiguous on this point. Early and appropriate intervention — taking the injury seriously from day one, providing the right care at the right time, communicating openly with the injured worker about what to expect — produces dramatically better outcomes and lower costs over the life of the claim. The cheapest claim is not the one you ignore. It's the one you handle well from the beginning.

But that requires the system to do something it's not very good at: treating every injury as if the person attached to it matters.

* * *

Seven Thousand Stories a Day

I mentioned in Chapter 1 that more than 7,000 Americans are newly injured on the job every single day. Let that number settle for a moment. Seven thousand. That's roughly the capacity of a mid-sized concert arena, filled to the rafters, every day. Five days a week, fifty-two weeks a year.

Each one of those 7,000 is a story. Some of them are straightforward — a fall, a treatment, a recovery, back to work in a few weeks. Some of them are complicated, involving multiple body parts, pre-existing conditions, disputed causation, and a recovery timeline that stretches well beyond anything the initial paperwork anticipated. Some of them are tragic, involving permanent impairment, lost careers, and lives that are never quite the same.

And every single one of them enters the same system. The same Rube Goldberg machine we talked about. The same forms, the same process, the same bureaucratic infrastructure that was originally designed for an industrial economy where the typical injury was a factory worker who broke an arm and needed six weeks off. That system now has to handle the warehouse worker with a repetitive stress disorder, the office employee with carpal tunnel syndrome, the nurse with a needle stick exposure, the firefighter with PTSD, and the construction worker who fell three stories — all with essentially the same playbook.

Meanwhile, the injured workers themselves are changing too. In 2015, in an article for the IAIABC Journal, I wrote that we were dealing with a workforce that is older, heavier, more sedentary, and more likely to have pre-existing chronic conditions than at any point in history. And today that workforce is a decade older and likely a few pounds heavier. Obesity alone is a ticking time bomb for the system. Over the past three decades, the United States has seen a doubling of obesity prevalence. Add in the dramatic rise in diabetes, decreased physical activity, and related complications, and you have a population of workers who are harder to heal and harder to return to function — not because they don't want to get better, but because the biological deck is increasingly stacked against them.

Workers' compensation cannot meet the demands of the future with the processes of the past. And that starts with how we think about the injury itself.

* * *

It's Not a Scratch. It's a Starting Line.

Under Workers' Recovery — the system this book is arguing for — the moment of injury is not the beginning of a claims process. It's the beginning of a recovery process. That distinction isn't semantic. It's foundational.

When an injury is the beginning of a claim, every incentive in the system aligns around managing the financial exposure. How much will this cost? How quickly can we close it? What are our reserves? The injured worker exists primarily as a line item.

When an injury is the beginning of a recovery, the questions change. What does this person need to heal? How do we get them the right care as quickly as possible? What are the barriers to their return to function — not just return to work, but return to the life they were living before that clock started ticking on their first day in the system?

Return to function. Remember that phrase. We'll come back to it throughout this book, because it is the beating heart of what Workers' Recovery is about. Every injured worker wants to pick up their child. Wants to walk the dog. Wants to bend down and smell the roses. Restoring those functions — those deeply human, deeply personal capabilities — is what drives genuine recovery. And from that foundation, return to work becomes a natural extension rather than an administrative mandate imposed from above.

But we're getting ahead of ourselves again. Before we can talk about recovery, we have to survive the employer's response. And that, as we'll see in the next chapter, is an adventure all its own.

In the meantime, the next time someone tells you it's just a scratch, or just a little bunny rabbit, you have my permission to be suspicious. The Killer Rabbit didn't look like much either. And those knights never saw it coming.

Chapter 3
Paperwork: The Second Injury

Somewhere in America right now, a person with a legitimate workplace injury is sitting at a kitchen table, staring at a stack of forms, wondering if this is some kind of test.

The First Report of Injury wants to know the "mechanism of injury." The claim form wants to know the "nature of injury." The employer's supplemental report wants to know the "cause of injury." These are, for the record, three different ways of asking what happened. The injured worker, who knows exactly what happened — "I fell off a ladder" — is now trying to figure out whether falling off a ladder is a mechanism, a nature, or a cause. It might be all three. It might be none. The forms aren't telling.

Meanwhile, the ice pack on their shoulder is melting.

* * *

A Brief History of Killing Trees

The workers' compensation system has been generating paperwork for over a century, and in that time it has elevated the practice to something approaching an art form. A dark, soul-crushing, entirely unnecessary art form, but an art form nonetheless.

When the first workers' compensation laws were enacted in the early 1900s, the paperwork was relatively simple. A worker got hurt. Someone wrote it down. A doctor examined them. Someone else wrote that down. Benefits were calculated and paid. It was bureaucracy, sure, but it was manageable bureaucracy. You could hold the entire paper trail in one hand and still have fingers free to make a rude gesture at it.

Then something happened. Actually, a lot of things happened. Legislatures added requirements. Regulators added forms. Insurers added documentation protocols. Attorneys added discovery requests. Medical providers added treatment authorization forms. And each time a new form or requirement was added, nobody thought to remove an old one. The paperwork didn't evolve. It accumulated. Like sedimentary rock, each era of reform deposited a new layer on top of the last, until what started as a simple reporting mechanism became a geological formation of bureaucracy.

And here's the truly remarkable part: we did all of this before computers. When the digital age arrived and promised to free us from paper, the workers' compensation system said, "Fantastic. Now we can generate paperwork even faster." And it did. We didn't eliminate the forms. We digitized them. Which means the injured worker sitting at that kitchen table is now staring at the same forms their grandparents filled out, only now they're in PDF format and the "submit" button doesn't work on their phone.

* * *

A Field Guide to the Forms

Let's take a tour of what an injured worker actually encounters and what their injury generates, paperwork-wise, in the first few days after an injury. Keep in mind that this varies by jurisdiction — because of course it does, there are over fifty of them, each with its own special flavor of bureaucratic creativity — but the general experience is remarkably consistent in its ability to make a bad day worse.

First, there's the **First Report of Injury**, sometimes called the Employer's First Report, which is the system's birth certificate for your claim. This document announces to the insurer that something happened to someone somewhere and that they'd like some help, please. It asks for the who, what, when, where, and how of the injury, along with your Social Security number, your date of birth, your hire date, your hourly wage, your average weekly wage, and your supervisor's name. Some versions also ask for your job title, which sounds simple until you realize that "whatever they need me to do" is not an option in the dropdown menu.

Then there may be the **Employee Claim Form**, which is the worker's own account of what happened. This is distinct from the Employer's First Report because apparently the same event needs to be documented from multiple perspectives, like a workplace injury version of the Rashomon effect. The claim form asks many of the same questions the First Report already asked, which gives the injured worker the comforting feeling that nobody is actually reading any of this.

Next comes the **Authorization for Medical Treatment**. In some states, the employer or insurer directs the injured worker to a specific physician or medical network. In others, the worker has free choice. In still others, it's free choice but only from an approved list, which is "free choice" in the same way that a multiple-choice test is "free thought." Regardless, there's a form for it. And the form needs to be filled out before treatment can begin, because nothing says "urgent medical care" quite like a mandatory administrative prerequisite.

From there, the paperwork multiplies like Tribbles on the Starship Enterprise. There are forms for wage verification, recorded statements, medical release authorizations, pharmacy benefit enrollment, and direct deposit authorizations. Of course, no claim is complete without return-to-work status forms and independent medical examination scheduling forms. And we would be remiss if we did not mention that in some jurisdictions, there are forms to request copies of the forms you've already filled out, because apparently the system doesn't trust itself either.

In fact, today the workers' comp systems of 50 US States, DC, Federal and Longshore, offer up a whopping library of more than 3,700 jurisdictional forms to manage the care of injured workers. They all come with their own requirements. Filing deadlines, digital signatures, wet signatures, support documentation, even font sizes in some cases; all must be properly curated lest the responsible entity runs afoul of the rules and risks being sent to bed without their supper. Or massive fines. Whatever. All of this despite the rise of Electronic Data Interchange, or EDI, which was intended to reduce paperwork and facilitate the rapid distribution of data to states and other entities that in many cases don't have a clue what to do with it. But they have it, and that is all that really matters. In today's workers' compensation ecosystem, it is adherence to paperwork and process that is important. Results are, unfortunately, a secondary concern.

* * *

Lost in Translation (And You're Not Even Speaking Another Language)

The forms themselves might be manageable if they were written in a language that human beings actually speak. They are not.

Workers' compensation paperwork exists in a linguistic uncanny valley somewhere between English and legal jargon, with occasional detours into medical terminology and insurance-speak. It is a dialect spoken fluently by approximately no one, including many of the professionals who work within the system.

Consider the injured worker — let's call him Dave — who hurt his back lifting boxes at a warehouse. Dave is in pain. Dave is worried about his job. Dave may or may not have graduated high school. Dave is now being asked to describe the "nature and extent of the disability" and identify the "specific body part or system affected." Dave's back hurts. Dave would like to write "my back hurts." The form would like something more clinical. Dave does not have anything more clinical. Dave and the form are at an impasse.

Now imagine Dave's experience if English is his second language. Or if Dave has limited literacy. Or if Dave is on pain medication that makes it hard to concentrate. Or if Dave is simply overwhelmed, frightened, and not in the frame of mind to parse the difference between "occurrence" and "accident" and "incident" — three words the system uses more or less interchangeably except when it doesn't, and the difference occasionally matters in ways that can affect whether Dave's claim gets paid.

And we cannot forget acronyms and industry jargon. No injury file is complete without at least one passing reference to MMI (which to the unaware means Maximum Medical Improvement). And we can bet dollars to donuts that many of the hard working, well meaning, workers' compensation professionals slogging through the regulatory maze of their industry have likely used the phrase MMI in a discussion with an injured worker, while never pausing to ask them if anyone ever bothered to explain what it actually meant (Hint: It doesn't mean what many injured workers think it means).

This is not a hypothetical problem. This is the daily reality for millions of workers. The system's own language creates a barrier to entry for the very people it's designed to serve. It's as if someone designed a life raft that required assembly instructions written in Sanskrit.

* * *

Fifty States, Fifty Systems, Infinite Headaches

Here's a fun wrinkle that deserves its own section: there is no single workers' compensation system in the United States. There are more than fifty. Each state has its own laws, its own forms, its own reporting requirements, its own deadlines, and its own idiosyncratic approach to what information is needed and when. Add in federal programs for federal employees, longshore workers, and a few other categories, and you've got a patchwork quilt that no rational person would have designed on purpose.

This means that a national employer — a company operating in, say, thirty states — is navigating thirty different sets of paperwork requirements. Thirty different First Report formats. Thirty different filing deadlines. Thirty different definitions of what constitutes a compensable injury. The report that's compliant in Ohio might be incomplete in Oregon. The deadline that gives you ten days in Texas gives you five in Tennessee. The form that asks for twelve data points in Michigan asks for twenty-seven in Massachusetts.

The IAIABC has spent decades working on standardization, including efforts to develop a common First Report of Injury (FROI). However, those efforts resulted in threats against the interlopers who dared to suggest any semblance of uniformity. And progress has been made (but not regarding a common FROI). But the fundamental reality remains: the system is a balkanized confederation of jurisdictions, each zealously protective of its own way of doing things, and the paperwork reflects that fragmentation with the fidelity of a mirror.

For the injured worker, this jurisdictional complexity is usually invisible. They fill out whatever forms are put in front of them and hope for the best. But for the employers, insurers, and third-party administrators trying to manage claims across state lines, it's a compliance nightmare that consumes enormous resources — resources that could, in a more sensible world, be spent on actually helping injured workers recover.

Remember that insurance carrier representative who said the claimant is no longer relevant to the process? This is part of why. When the process itself becomes this complex, managing the process takes precedence over managing the person. The paperwork becomes the job. The injured worker becomes an afterthought. Again.

* * *

Tell Me Again. No, Really. Again.

If there is one feature of workers' compensation paperwork that stands above all others in its capacity to drive people to the brink, it is the relentless, unyielding, almost weaponized redundancy.

The injured worker provides their account of the injury on the First Report. Then again on the Employee Claim Form. Then again to the adjuster during a recorded statement. Then again to the treating physician. Then again to the IME doctor. Then again on the disability status form. Then again if there's an appeal. Then again if there's a deposition. The same story, told and retold and documented and re-documented, as if the system is hoping that the seventh retelling will produce a different version and they can finally cry "Gotcha!"

This isn't just annoying. It's actively harmful. Every time an injured worker has to recount their injury, they're reliving it. Every retelling reinforces the pain narrative. Every form that asks them to describe their limitations reminds them of what they can't do. The system, in its obsessive quest to document the injury from every conceivable angle, is inadvertently reinforcing the very identity — injured, limited, disabled — that stands between the worker and recovery.

Remember what we discussed about words and their power? Every form that asks "describe your disability" is reinforcing the concept of disability. Every questionnaire that catalogs limitations is building a mental inventory of things the worker can't do. The paperwork isn't just documenting the situation. It's shaping it. And it's shaping it in exactly the wrong direction.

Under Workers' Recovery, the question wouldn't be "describe your disability." It would be "what functions would you most like to restore?" Same information, gathered with a fundamentally different orientation. One points toward limitation. The other points toward a goal. But that's a revolutionary concept in a system that has spent a century perfecting the art of documentation and approximately zero time questioning whether the documentation itself might be part of the problem.

* * *

Death by a Thousand Paper Cuts

There is a concept in workers' compensation called the "secondary injury." Traditionally, this refers to a subsequent physical injury or complication arising from the original one. But I'd argue that the biggest secondary injury in the system isn't physical at all. It's administrative.

The paperwork itself is injuring people. Not with sharp edges — though if you've ever handled a stack of NCR forms, you know the risk is real — but through the cumulative psychological weight of a process that feels designed to exhaust rather than assist. Every form is a reminder that you're in the system. Every request for documentation is a reminder that the system doesn't trust you. Every week that passes while paperwork sits in someone's queue is a week that recovery isn't progressing.

I've talked to injured workers who describe the claims process as more stressful than the injury itself. Think about that. People who have experienced genuine physical trauma — broken bones, torn ligaments, surgical procedures — and who, when asked about their worst experience, point not to the moment of injury but to the months of paperwork that followed. The body healed. The bureaucracy harmed.

And for the workers who lack education, language skills, or a strong support system, the paperwork isn't just stressful. It's a wall. An impenetrable, jargon-laden, form-filled wall that separates them from the benefits and care they're legally entitled to. Some give up. Some never file at all. Some accept settlements that are a fraction of what they deserve because the alternative is more paperwork, more forms, more of the system that has already taken more from them than the injury did.

The great compromise was supposed to be simple. You get hurt, you get help. We've buried that simplicity under a mountain of paper and called it "due process."

* * *

What a Grown-Up System Would Look Like

I'm not naive enough to suggest we can eliminate paperwork from the workers' compensation system. There are legitimate reasons for documentation. Fraud prevention, regulatory compliance, medical coordination, legal protections for both employers and employees — these are real needs, and they require some degree of record-keeping.

But there's a vast difference between documentation that serves the people and documentation that serves the system. A grown-up system — a Workers' Recovery system — would start with a radical question: does this form help the injured worker get better? If the answer is no, the form needs to justify its existence or disappear.

A single, standardized First Report of Injury that works across all jurisdictions. We've been talking about this for decades. It's time to stop talking. The technology exists. The data standards exist. The political will is the only thing that's missing, and that's a choice, not a constraint.

Plain language on every form. Not legal language. Not insurance language. Not medical language. Language that Dave, our warehouse worker with the bad back, can read and understand without a translator. If a form can't be understood by the average person it's being given to, the form has failed, not the person.

One-time data entry. You tell your story once. The system captures it once. Every subsequent form, report, and communication pulls from that single source. No more Rashomon effect. No more telling the same story seven times to seven different people. One story, properly documented, accessible to everyone who needs it.

And here's the real revolutionary idea: forms that are oriented toward recovery, not just documentation. Instead of cataloging what's wrong, they would also capture what's possible. What functions does the worker want to restore? What activities matter most to them? What does success look like from their perspective? This isn't soft thinking. It's smart design. When you build the goal into the intake process, you orient the entire system toward that goal from the very first form. And you get buy-in from the injured worker themselves.

The paperwork in workers' compensation doesn't have to be the second injury. It could be the first step toward getting better. But only if we stop treating it as an end in itself and start treating it as what it should be: a tool in service of the person behind the claim number.

Speaking of people behind the claim number, in the next chapter we'll explore what happens when that person turns to their employer for support and discovers that the response ranges from genuinely wonderful to spectacularly unhelpful — sometimes within the same company, on the same day, depending on which manager picks up the phone.

Chapter 4
The Employer Shuffle

The phone call comes on a Tuesday afternoon. Your employee — let's call her Maria — hurt her shoulder on the production line. The shift supervisor is on the other end, sounding like someone who has just been asked to defuse a bomb using only a paperclip and an employee handbook.

"So… Maria says her shoulder popped. She's in the break room. What do I do?"

What happens next will depend on who picks up that call. If it's someone trained, empathetic, and competent, Maria's recovery starts right now — with the right words, the right response, and the right care. If it's someone untrained, overwhelmed, or working from a playbook written by the legal department in 1997, Maria's recovery may have just hit its first significant obstacle. And she hasn't even left the break room yet.

* * *

The Good, the Bad, and the "Please Don't Sue Us"

Employer responses to workplace injuries exist on a spectrum so wide it would make a rainbow jealous. On one end, you have companies that handle injuries with genuine compassion, clear communication, and a well-oiled process that prioritizes the worker's wellbeing. On the other end, you have companies whose response to an injured employee can best be described as a panicked attempt to make the problem go away before anyone notices, preferably without spending money or admitting that anything happened.

Most employers live somewhere in the vast, bewildered middle. They don't mean to handle injuries poorly. They just... don't know how to handle them well. Nobody taught them. Their training, to the extent they received any, consisted of being shown where the incident report forms are kept and being told to call the 800 number on the insurance card. That's the workers' compensation equivalent of learning to swim by being handed a pamphlet about water.

The result is a lottery. Whether an injured worker gets a supportive response or a hostile one depends less on company policy and more on which supervisor happens to be on duty, how that supervisor is feeling, and whether the supervisor personally likes the injured worker. The jurisdiction where the injury occurs can also affect these lottery odds. A few states have established a focused support system encouraging recovery and return to work. Most do not. This is not a system. This is a coin flip with consequences.

* * *

The First Five Minutes (Where Everything Is Won or Lost)

There is a body of research that would fill a small library demonstrating that the employer's initial response to a workplace injury is one of the single greatest predictors of claim outcome. Not the severity of the injury. Not the quality of the medical care. The employer's response. Those first few minutes after an injury is reported set the trajectory for everything that follows.

When an employer responds with genuine concern — "Are you okay? Let's get you to a doctor. Don't worry about the paperwork right now. Your health comes first" — something remarkable happens. The injured worker's stress level drops. Their trust in the process increases. Their perception of pain, believe it or not, can actually decrease. They feel valued, supported, and motivated to recover. The science on this is not ambiguous. How you respond to an injury matters as much as how you treat it.

When an employer responds with suspicion, annoyance, or bureaucratic indifference — "Fill out this form. We need to investigate. Are you sure this happened at work? Can you finish your shift?" — the opposite happens. Stress increases. Trust evaporates. The adversarial dynamic that will poison the entire claim is established in the first conversation. The injured worker goes from "my employer cares about me" to "my employer thinks I'm lying" in the time it takes a supervisor to raise an eyebrow.

And here's what makes this genuinely tragic: most employers who respond badly don't do it out of malice. They do it out of ignorance. They've never been trained in how to respond to an injury. Nobody told them that the words they choose in those first five minutes will echo through every phase of the claim. Nobody explained that "Are you sure this happened at work?" — a question that feels perfectly reasonable from a due-diligence perspective — sounds like an accusation of fraud to a person who is hurt, scared, and vulnerable. The road to a litigation-plagued, eighteen-month claim is paved with good intentions and bad training.

* * *

The Supervisor: Untrained, Unprepared, Unavoidable

The front-line supervisor is, in most organizations, the single most important person in the workers' compensation process. They are the first point of contact. They set the tone. They are the face of the company at the moment when the injured worker is forming their first impressions of how this is going to go.

And overwhelmingly, they are completely unprepared for this role.

Most supervisors were promoted because they were good at the work, not because they were good at managing the human complications that arise when the work goes wrong. They know how to run a production line, manage a crew, or hit a quota. They do not know how to talk to a frightened employee about medical treatment options, explain the claims process in reassuring terms, or navigate the psychological minefield of workplace injury without accidentally detonating something.

What training they do receive tends to fall into one of two categories. The first is the "legal compliance" model, in which a supervisor is taught the minimum required steps to avoid regulatory trouble: report the injury within the required timeframe, direct the employee to the appropriate medical provider, fill out the correct forms. This produces supervisors who are technically compliant and emotionally useless — people who can check every box on the incident report while making the injured worker feel like a problem to be processed.

The second is the "cost containment" model, in which the supervisor is taught, explicitly or implicitly, that injuries are expensive and should be minimized whenever possible. This produces supervisors who discourage reporting, suggest that minor injuries don't need medical attention, and communicate — through a thousand subtle signals — that getting hurt at work is an inconvenience the company would rather not deal with. We met these folks back in Chapter 2, cheerfully assuring the knights that everything was fine, the little bunny was not a concern. Their hearts may be in the right place. Their training is not.

There is another area of concern here that has less to do with proper training and everything to do with the law of unintended consequences. Sometimes well-meaning programs such as safety incentives and bonuses tied to workplace safety lead to very poor injury response. A program that rewards staff for a certain period of accident-free days can result in very negative peer pressure, or the loss of a bonus due to a lost time claim can negatively affect how supervisors respond to a newly reported injury.

I can honestly say I've lived that latter scenario. Having been raised in a family-owned restaurant, I went into restaurant management after graduating college. My initial job was with a large, self-insured employer, and our quarterly bonuses were tied to, among other things, workplace injury rates and lost time claims. Typical of the managers I mention here, I did not know much about workers' comp in those days. All I knew was when I had a lost time claim some guy named Frank Gates would gig my operating statement 50 Grand for something called a "reserve." I didn't know Frank, but I didn't like him. And with that reserve hit, my bonus would be gone. And looking back, I wasn't particularly thrilled with my injured workers. Education about workers' comp would have benefited all involved.

What's almost entirely absent from supervisor training is the one thing that matters most: how to be a human being talking to another human being who is hurt and scared. How to express genuine concern. How to communicate clearly about what happens next without triggering fear or defensiveness. How to maintain a relationship with the injured worker throughout their recovery. These aren't soft skills. They're the skills that determine whether a claim costs $5,000 or $500,000.

* * *

The Scarlet "C" (C Is for Claim)

Let's talk about something that everyone in the workers' compensation industry knows exists but nobody likes to discuss in polite company: the stigma of filing a claim.

The moment a worker files a workers' compensation claim, something shifts in the social dynamics of the workplace. It's subtle, mostly. A change in how coworkers interact with them. A coolness from the supervisor. The sense of being watched more carefully, evaluated more critically, trusted less. In Chapter 2 we called the injured worker a "pariah" — and while that word may seem strong, talk to enough injured workers and you'll hear stories that justify it.

Some of this stigma is driven by suspicion. There is a persistent belief, particularly among certain employers and supervisors, that a significant percentage of workers' compensation claims are fraudulent. The data does not support this belief. Study after study has shown that fraud rates in workers' compensation are low — generally estimated at between one and two percent of claims. But the perception of widespread fraud persists, and it colors how injured workers are treated from the moment they report.

Some of the stigma is driven by resentment. When an employee is out on a claim, their work doesn't disappear. It gets redistributed to their coworkers, who are now doing more with less. The absent worker becomes, in the eyes of the team, the reason everyone else is working harder. This is not rational — the worker didn't choose to get hurt — but resentment rarely consults the facts before settling in.

And some of the stigma is driven by the employer's own behavior. When management treats a claim as a cost event rather than a human event, that attitude permeates the organization. When supervisors are evaluated, formally or informally, on the number of claims in their department, they develop an allergic reaction to injury reports. As previously noted, there are some situations where the supervisor's compensation is affected by losses among those he or she supervises. When the company's response to a claim is visibly adversarial — surveillance, recorded statements, IME referrals that feel punitive — it sends a message to every worker in the building: if you get hurt here, you're on your own.

Consider this point. If a person falls off a ladder at home and is hurt, co-workers and management are likely to show compassion. They may call or visit. Send flowers. Bring food. When that ladder was at work, it is a completely different scenario, and the reaction makes a difference.

The injured worker absorbs all of this. And it becomes another barrier to recovery, as real and as damaging as the injury itself.

* * *

The Silence Is Deafening (And Expensive)

If there is one thing I could change about the employer's role in workers' compensation tomorrow — one single thing that would produce the greatest improvement in outcomes for the least amount of effort — it would be this: communication.

The typical employer's communication with an injured worker follows a depressingly predictable pattern. In the immediate aftermath of the injury, there's a flurry of contact — forms to sign, statements to give, appointments to schedule. Then, once the initial reporting is done and the claim has been handed off to the insurer, the employer goes silent. Weeks pass. Sometimes months. The worker hears from the adjuster, the doctor, the pharmacy, the utilization review nurse, and approximately seventeen automated reminder systems. From their employer — the organization they worked for, the people they saw every day, the place that was their professional home – they hear nothing.

Nature abhors a vacuum, and so does the human mind. When information is absent, imagination fills the gap. And imagination, when you're injured and anxious, is not your friend. The worker begins to wonder. Do they still have a job? Has their position been filled? Does anyone care? Are they being forgotten? Are they being replaced? Is the company building a case to let them go?

These fears may be completely unfounded. The employer may fully intend to welcome the worker back. But they haven't said that. And in the absence of reassurance, anxiety grows. And anxiety, as we know, actively impedes recovery. It increases pain perception, reduces motivation, extends disability duration, and makes the worker far more susceptible to the advice of the attorney who conveniently shows up in the mailbox offering to "protect their rights."

I've been told of some employers who believe once a workers' compensation claim has been filed, that they are no longer permitted to speak to them. Nothing could be further from the truth. In fact, the exact opposite of silence is called for. And that does not change if an employee hires an attorney. At such a point they may no longer discuss the particulars of the case without the attorney present, but they certainly can continue to communicate. They can ask how they're feeling. They can ask if they need anything. They can even bring them up to speed at what is happening in the workplace, helping them still feel connected to a place that has major significance to them. They can, through the simple act of communication, show them that they care.

It is critical to know this: In the absence of clear and open communication, cancerous thoughts will grow. And it is those cancerous thoughts, what is going on in the mind of the injured worker, that are far more likely to derail recovery, much more so than the physical injury itself.

The industry's traditional "three points of contact" standard was supposed to address this. The idea was simple: the adjuster, the employer, and the medical provider would all stay in touch with the injured worker. In practice, "contact" devolved into leaving a voicemail message and checking a box. Leaving a message on someone's answering machine should never be considered "contact." But by default, it has become the industry's minimum standard – which says everything you need to know about the industry's standards.

* * *

Light Duty: Where Dignity May Go to Die

At some point during the recovery process, the conversation turns to "light duty." This is the employer's attempt to bring the injured worker back to the workplace in a limited capacity while they continue to heal. It is, in concept, a perfectly reasonable idea. Staying connected to work, maintaining routines, contributing meaningfully – all of these things support recovery. The research is clear on this.

The execution, however, is where things get interesting.

There are employers who believe that counting paper clips is a viable job for someone returning with restrictions. Others assign the injured worker to sit in a room and watch training videos for eight hours — the same training videos, on repeat, day after day, like a corporate Groundhog Day designed by someone who has never actually seen Groundhog Day. Still others create "make-work" positions so transparently pointless that the injured worker spends more energy pretending to be useful than they would doing their actual job.

The message these assignments send is not subtle: we don't really want you here. We're not investing in your recovery. We're parking you in a corner until we figure out what to do with you, or until you get frustrated enough to quit, whichever comes first.

Every person needs to have value — a useful, contributory role in society. That should be obvious to all, but it is unfortunately not the case. The injured worker who is assigned to count paper clips doesn't feel like they're recovering. They feel like they're being punished. And punishment is not, it turns out, a clinically effective recovery strategy.

Meaningful light duty — work that is genuinely within the worker's restrictions, contributes to the operation, and makes the worker feel valued — is one of the most powerful recovery tools available. It keeps the worker engaged, maintains their identity as a contributing member of the team, and creates a natural bridge back to full duty. But it requires thought, creativity, and a genuine belief that the injured worker is worth the effort. That last part is where many employers fall short.

* * *

What the Good Ones Get Right

I've spent a lot of this chapter cataloging the ways employers get it wrong, which is fair and necessary but also incomplete. Because some employers get it spectacularly right, and they deserve attention too — not just as a counterbalance, but as a blueprint.

The employers who excel at managing workplace injuries share a set of common characteristics. They train their supervisors not just in compliance, but in communication. They treat the first five minutes after an injury report as the most critical intervention in the entire claim. They maintain regular, genuine contact with injured workers throughout their recovery — not because a procedure manual tells them to, but because they understand that the worker is still a member of the team, even when they're not in the building.

They educate their workforce to eliminate stigma. They don't punish injury reporting; they encourage it. They create light duty assignments that are meaningful and dignified. They involve the injured worker's supervisor in recovery planning, not as a watchdog but as an advocate. And they measure success not in claim costs but in return-to-function outcomes.

These companies exist. I've seen them. I've talked to their risk managers and their injured workers. And the results are consistent: lower claim costs, shorter durations, fewer litigated claims, higher employee retention, and — this is the part that should matter most — injured workers who actually get better, who return to productive lives, and who speak well of the company that took care of them when they were at their most vulnerable.

It's not magic. It's not even complicated. It's just a commitment to treating the person behind the claim number as a person.

* * *

From Injury to Recovery: A Simple Employer Roadmap

At the moment of injury:

- Lead with concern, not paperwork. "Are you okay?" should always come before "Fill this out."
- Get the worker appropriate medical attention immediately — don't delay care for administrative convenience.
- Let the worker know they are valued and that their job is secure (assuming it is). Say it explicitly. Don't assume they know.
- Avoid investigative language in the first conversation. Questions about causation can wait. Compassion can't.

In the first 48 hours:

- Report the claim promptly and accurately — delays in reporting create delays in care.
- Assign a single internal point of contact so the worker knows exactly who to call with questions.

- Contact the worker at home to check on them. A genuine phone call — not a text, not an email — goes further than most employers realize.
- Communicate clearly about what happens next: who their adjuster will be, what the process looks like, and what the expected timeline is. Uncertainty breeds anxiety; information reduces it.

During recovery:

- Maintain regular, genuine communication. Call to ask how they're doing, not just when they're coming back.
- Include the worker's spouse or partner in communications where appropriate — they are a critical influence on recovery.
- Regarding catastrophic claims, understand that communication with the spouse is exceptionally important in those cases.
- Keep the worker connected to the workplace. Share team news, invite them to non-mandatory gatherings, remind them they're still part of the team.
- Never go silent. If there's nothing new to report, call and say that. The absence of information is never interpreted as good news.

When preparing for return to work:

- Design light duty assignments that are meaningful, dignified, and genuinely within medical restrictions.
- Involve the worker in the planning — ask them what they think they can do, not just what the doctor's note allows.

- Prepare the team. Brief supervisors and coworkers so the return isn't awkward, and address any resentment or stigma directly.
- Focus on return to function, not just return to the building. A worker who is back at their desk but not genuinely contributing is not recovering — they're just present.

Throughout the entire process:

- Treat the claim as a human event, not a cost event. The financial metrics will follow the human ones.
- Don't stop communicating because an attorney is involved. You may not discuss case specifics without the attorney present, but you can — and should — continue to express care and maintain the relationship.
- Document your good faith efforts. Not because you need to cover yourself legally (though you might), but because a record of genuine engagement is the best defense against litigation you'll never need.
- Remember: the injured worker didn't choose to get hurt. Respond the way you'd want your own employer to respond if it happened to you.

* * *

The Four Points of Communication

Under Workers' Recovery, the employer's role transforms from passive participant to active partner in recovery. And at the center of that transformation is a concept I've been advocating for years: the Four Points of Communication.

The traditional three points of contact — adjuster, employer, medical provider — failed because it was built around the system, not the person. The Four Points of Communication is built around the recovering worker. It requires actual two-way communication, not voicemails into the void. And it adds a critical fourth point that the current system ignores entirely: the worker's spouse, partner, or support network.

This isn't a radical idea. It's a recognition of what every health care professional already knows: recovery doesn't happen in isolation. The people closest to the injured worker have an enormous influence on their mindset, their motivation, and their recovery trajectory. A spouse who is scared and uninformed can inadvertently reinforce fear and dependency. A spouse who is included, educated, and reassured becomes a powerful ally in the recovery process. The current system pretends this person doesn't exist. Workers' Recovery puts them at the table.

Employers should be educated to avoid the stigma of workplace injury for their employees. Supervisors should be required — not encouraged, required — to reach out and maintain communications with their recovering workers. Co-workers should be encouraged to do the same. A well-trained Recovery Specialist with an adequate workload could facilitate this entire process. But that requires training, investment, and a philosophical commitment to the idea that the injured worker is still a member of the team.

Which brings us, inevitably, to the question of who's actually managing this claim on the other end of the phone. In the next chapter, we'll enter the world of insurance — where hope goes to hold, where denials can be issued with the efficiency of a factory assembly line, and where the concept of "customer service" is sometimes applied with all the warmth and sincerity of an automated phone tree.

Your call is very important to us. Please continue to hold.

Chapter 5
Insurance: Where Hope Goes to Hold

The letter arrives on a Thursday. It is printed on insurance company letterhead in a font that suggests authority without warmth — the typographic equivalent of a firm handshake from someone who doesn't make eye contact. It is likely written by a skilled team of attorneys; and is easily understood – by any other team of skilled attorneys.

"Dear Claimant," it begins. Not "Dear Maria." Not "Dear Ms. Rodriguez." Dear Claimant. You are no longer a person with a name. You are a category.

The letter informs you that your claim has been received and is under review. It provides a claim number, which you should reference in all future correspondence. It lists the name of your adjuster, a phone number, and office hours. It does not mention hope, healing, or any word that might suggest the insurance company is interested in your recovery as opposed to your file. It does, however, include a paragraph about your obligation to cooperate with the investigation, which is a lovely way to welcome someone into a system ostensibly designed to help them.

Welcome to the insurance phase. Thank you for holding.

* * *

Meet Your Adjuster (If You Can Reach Them)

The claims adjuster is, in theory, the injured worker's primary point of contact within the insurance system. They are the person assigned to manage your claim, coordinate your benefits, authorize your treatment, and generally serve as the human face of a process that would otherwise be entirely faceless. They are, in the parlance of the industry, your "claims professional."

In practice, they are the person whose voicemail you will get to know intimately.

This is not, in most cases, the adjuster's fault. The average workers' compensation claims adjuster is managing a caseload that would make an air traffic controller weep. We're talking 200, 250, sometimes 300 or more active claims at any given time. Each of those claims is a person with an injury, a medical history, an employer, a set of state-specific regulations, a treatment plan, a return-to-work timeline, and an ever-growing file that needs to be documented, reviewed, and acted upon. Now multiply that by 250 and try to return a phone call.

At 250 claims, an adjuster could spend exactly 1.92 minutes per claim per day in an eight-hour shift, assuming they never eat lunch, never attend a meeting, never use the restroom, and never pause to question their career choices. In reality, a significant portion of their day is consumed by documentation requirements, internal compliance reviews, supervisor check-ins, and the sheer administrative weight of managing a caseload that no human being can reasonably manage. The time left for actually talking to injured workers — you know, the ostensible purpose of the job — is whatever scraps remain after the system has fed.

The result is predictable and depressing. The injured worker calls their adjuster. The adjuster is on another call, in a meeting, at lunch, or buried under the paperwork generated by their other 249 claims. The call goes to voicemail. The injured worker leaves a message. The adjuster, when they finally surface for air, sees seventeen voicemails, triages by urgency, and returns the ones that are on fire. The others wait. The injured worker, meanwhile, is sitting at home, wondering why nobody will call them back, slowly marinating in the anxiety and frustration that we know — from everything we've discussed in previous chapters — actively impedes recovery.

We must pause here and say something important: most claims adjusters are good people doing an impossible job. And in many organizations, they simply do not get the respect they deserve. Many years ago, in a discussion with an industry friend a statement was made that reflects that reality. We were talking about a recent promotion of another individual within a different company. My acquaintance, an attorney, was somewhat perplexed at the selection of this person. She said, "I don't know why they chose him. He's just a claims guy." With only a few years under my belt in the industry at this point, the comment surprised me, and I honestly did not understand it. It wasn't until I relayed that question to another industry friend, someone with years of experience in claims, that I was given a clear understanding. He told me that in many organizations, the claims department is viewed simply as an expense. It does not produce revenue and therefore is not given the attention and gravitas that other divisions might receive.

To this day, that is, by far, the stupidest thing I have ever heard within this industry.

Claims people are the front line in customer service, and at the most critical point of the business relationship; when someone is hurt and assets are at risk. How could anyone in their right mind minimize the importance of that position? It is the equivalent of General Motors deciding that cars are simply an expense and don't deserve any quality development. Of course, given my experience with GM in the 1980's and swearing to never again purchase their products, it may be an inappropriate comparison that also proves my point.

Claims people entered this profession, in many cases, because they genuinely wanted to help. They did not sign up to be a voicemail machine or spend their day putting fires out at their desk. The system itself has turned them into reactive rather than proactive workers. And we'll get to how Workers' Recovery would fix that. But first, we need to talk about training — or more accurately, the lack thereof.

* * *

Training: A Comedy in One Act

A 2013 industry study asked a simple question: "Does your organization have a formal training program for new hire claims staff with little or no experience?" The results were illuminating in the worst possible way. Forty-two percent of respondents answered yes. Thirty-seven percent answered no. The remaining nineteen percent said the question was not applicable. Setting aside the nineteen percent who apparently don't hire new people (a business model I have questions about), the percentage of applicable respondents who answered "no" jumps to an astonishing forty-seven percent.

Let that settle. Nearly half of the organizations in the workers' compensation insurance industry do not have a formal training program for new claims staff. Nearly half.

To put this in perspective: your barista went through more formal training to make your latte than many claims adjusters received before being handed a caseload of human beings in crisis. Your dog groomer has a certification process. The person who cuts your hair needs a state license. But the person responsible for managing the medical care, financial benefits, and recovery trajectory of an injured worker? In many organizations, they get a desk, a phone, a login, and a hearty "good luck."

The training that does exist tends to focus on the technical and regulatory aspects of the job: how to set reserves, how to comply with state-specific filing deadlines, how to navigate the claims management software without accidentally deleting someone's file. What is almost universally absent is training in the thing that matters most: how to communicate with an injured human being. How to set expectations. How to convey empathy through a phone line. How to explain a denial in a way that doesn't make the injured worker feel like they've been mugged by their employer's insurance company.

The industry has, in effect, built a system that demands emotional intelligence from professionals it has never bothered to train in emotional intelligence. Then it wonders why injured workers feel adversarial toward their adjusters. This is the equivalent of hiring a chef, teaching them only how to operate the cash register, and then being surprised when the soufflé doesn't rise.

* * *

The Art of Saying No (With a Form Letter)

If there is one moment in the workers' compensation process that crystallizes everything wrong with the current system, it is the denial letter.

The denial letter is a small masterpiece of bureaucratic communication. It manages to convey, in a single page, that your claim has been reviewed, your injury has been considered, and the insurance company has determined that it will not be covering your care. It often does this using language so dense with legal and regulatory terminology that the average reader needs a law degree, a medical dictionary, and a bottle of vodka to decode it. It references statutes by number, cites policy provisions by subsection, and deploys the phrase "based upon our review of the available evidence" with the casual authority of someone who has just performed a thorough investigation rather than, in many cases, glanced at an incomplete file between bites of a desk lunch.

The letter then helpfully informs you of your right to appeal, which is the system's way of saying, "We said no, but you're welcome to spend several more months asking us to reconsider while we continue not paying your medical bills." The appeal process, in most jurisdictions, involves additional paperwork, additional medical documentation, additional time, and additional stress — all of which are borne by the person who is, lest we forget, injured.

Not all denials are wrong. Let's be clear about that. Some claims are legitimately not compensable. Some don't meet the statutory requirements. Some involve injuries that genuinely aren't work-related. The system needs the ability to say no. The problem is not that denials exist. The problem is how they're deployed, how they're communicated, and how often they're used as a cost management tool rather than a legitimate determination of compensability.

For the injured worker on the receiving end, a denial is not an administrative event. It is a gut punch. It says: we don't believe you, or we don't care, or both. It says: you are on your own. And it frequently arrives at the exact moment when the worker is at their most vulnerable — in pain, out of work, uncertain about the future, and now told that the safety net they were promised under the Great Compromise has a rather large hole in it.

* * *

Press 1 for Frustration, Press 2 for Despair

We should talk about the phone system. Not because it's the most important thing wrong with workers' compensation insurance, but because it is the most universally experienced and the most viscerally infuriating, and because it is a perfect metaphor for everything else.

You are an injured worker. You have a question about your claim. You dial the number on the letter — the one that said "please contact your adjuster if you have any questions." What follows is a journey through the seven circles of automated telephony.

First, there's the greeting, delivered by a recorded voice so professionally warm that you almost believe a real person is talking to you. "Thank you for calling. Your call is important to us." This is the first fib. If your call were important, a person would answer it.

Then the menu. Press 1 for English. Press 2 for Spanish. Press 3 if you know your party's extension, which you don't, because your adjuster's extension was not included on the letter that told you to call. Press 4 for claims. You press 4. A new menu appears, like a hydra growing additional heads. Press 1 for new claims. Press 2 for existing claims. Press 3 for pharmacy. Press 4 for billing. Press 5 for "all other inquiries," which is the system's catch-all for "we ran out of buttons."

You press 2. You enter your claim number, which is fourteen digits long and which you have been told to reference in all correspondence but have not memorized because you are a human being, not a barcode scanner. You mistype it. The system asks you to try again. You try again. The system says "please hold while I transfer you to the next available representative."

Music plays. It is the kind of music that was specifically designed to be inoffensive, and in achieving total inoffensiveness has achieved a kind of aggressive blandness that is, in its own way, profoundly offensive. It is interrupted every ninety seconds by a recorded voice reminding you that your call is important. This is the second, third, fourth, fifth, and sixth fib.

Thirty-three minutes later, a person answers. They are not your adjuster. They are a general representative who can "pull up your file" and "leave a message for your adjuster." You have now spent twenty-three minutes on hold to leave a message you could have left on voicemail in thirty seconds, which you probably already did, which is why you called the main number in the first place.

This experience, repeated dozens of times over the life of a claim, does something to a person. It erodes trust. It reinforces the feeling that you are not important, that your recovery is not a priority, and that the system is designed to be navigated by it, not by you. It is, in miniature, the entire problem with workers' compensation insurance: a system built for the convenience of the institution rather than the needs of the human being it is supposed to serve.

That last sentence is one that bears remembering, as it encapsulates one of the major problems with today's workers' compensation system, a problem that permeates the industry across multiple stakeholders. I was once discussing the website traffic at my company with a plaintiff's attorney (or in California parlance, an Applicant's Attorney). He asked how many injured workers were visiting the site, and told me that "injured workers were critical, because they were the oil that lets the machine run."

What a fascinating and telling comment. He didn't portray the injured worker riding comfortably inside the vehicle designed to carry them to recovery. No, he put the injured worker inside the engine, lubricating the machine that was supposed to exist for them. And we all know what we do with oil that has outlived its usefulness. We dispose of it and get new oil. The encounter truly presented the question, does the machine exist for the injured worker, or does the injured worker now simply exist for the machine?

* * *

The Cost Containment Trap

At its core, the tension within workers' compensation insurance is simple: insurers are in the business of managing financial risk, and injured workers are in the business of trying to get better. These two objectives are not inherently incompatible, but the system has developed as though they are.

The push for discounts in medical networks and the focus on fee-for-service is resulting in a counterintuitive reality: injured workers may not be getting the best care, and the cheapest care may not be so inexpensive over the long haul. I once attended a conference where a Johns Hopkins physician cited research done by a US workers' compensation carrier that found 80 percent of their medical spend was being generated by 7 percent of the doctors in their network. Let that number sink in. Eighty percent of the money. Seven percent of the doctors. Something is deeply wrong with how we're selecting and compensating physicians in this system.

The logic of cost containment says: find the cheapest provider. The logic of recovery says: find the best provider. These are often not the same person. A doctor who charges more per visit but gets the worker back to function in six weeks is dramatically cheaper than a doctor who charges less per visit but keeps the worker in treatment for six months. But the system's metrics are built around per-visit cost, not outcomes. It's like judging a restaurant solely by the price of the ingredients without ever tasting the food.

This same logic infects every corner of the insurance process. Utilization review — the process by which an insurance company decides whether a proposed treatment is "medically necessary" — was designed as a quality control mechanism. In practice, it often functions as a cost control mechanism. The treating physician recommends an MRI. The utilization review nurse, who has never examined the patient and may or may not have relevant specialist expertise, determines it's not medically necessary. The MRI is denied. The physician appeals. The appeal takes weeks. Weeks of treatment delay, weeks of continued pain, weeks of recovery time lost — all to save the cost of an MRI that will probably be approved on appeal anyway.

The system is penny-wise and pound-catastrophically-foolish. And the pounds, as always, are being paid by the injured worker in the currency of delayed recovery, and the employer in the form of lengthened indemnity and potential litigation.

* * *

From Claims Adjuster to Recovery Specialist

Under Workers' Recovery, the claims adjuster doesn't disappear. They evolve. Adjusters would become Recovery Specialists. Claims Departments would become Recovery Management Divisions. And while the folks in subrogation might need to find new titles — sorry, subrogation, but "recovery" is taken — the real change isn't in the name. It's in the mission.

A Recovery Specialist's primary metric would not be cost containment. It would be return to function. Their caseloads would need to be dramatically reduced — because you cannot facilitate genuine recovery for 250 people simultaneously any more than you can have 250 meaningful conversations in a single day. Better training would be mandatory, not optional, and that training would emphasize communication, empathy, and recovery-oriented case management alongside the technical and regulatory fundamentals.

Naysayers — and there are always naysayers — will point to the cost. Smaller caseloads mean more staff. More training means more investment. Recovery-oriented metrics mean measuring things that are harder to quantify than dollars saved.

To which I say: do the math on the other side. What does it cost when a claim that should have resolved in eight weeks drags on for eighteen months because the adjuster was too overloaded to return a phone call? What does it cost when an injured worker hires an attorney because they felt ignored, and the claim that would have settled for $15,000 now costs $150,000? What does it cost when a worker who could have been returned to function ends up on permanent disability because nobody had the time, training, or institutional incentive to guide them toward recovery?

The most expensive claims adjuster in the world is the cheap one with 300 files on their desk and no training in how to talk to a human being. The industry just hasn't figured out how to put that on a spreadsheet yet.

* * *

Selecting Doctors: Outcome Over Discount

While we're reforming the insurance side of the equation, let's talk about how we choose the doctors who treat injured workers. Because the current approach — selecting physicians primarily on the basis of discounted fee schedules — is like choosing a pilot based on their lowest salary requirements. It works great right up until it doesn't.

Physicians in a Workers' Recovery system would be selected on the merits of their performance and paid on the basis of their outcomes. This is not an alien concept. The broader healthcare system has been inching toward value-based care for years. Workers' compensation is, characteristically, several inches behind.

The implementation is straightforward: track treatment durations and outcomes by physician. Doctors who consistently return workers to function quickly and without re-injury, even at a higher per-visit cost, should be preferred and rewarded. Doctors who keep patients in treatment indefinitely without demonstrable progress should be identified and, if the pattern persists, removed from the network. This is not about punishing doctors. It's about rewarding the ones who are actually good at what we need them to do: help people get better.

The data to do this already exists. Every insurer tracks medical costs, treatment durations, and return-to-work dates. The problem is that this data is used primarily to identify expensive claims, not effective doctors. Flipping that lens — from "who costs the most" to "who heals the best" — would be one of the single most impactful changes the insurance industry could make.

* * *

Hanging Up the Phone

The insurance industry is not the villain of this story, much as it might be satisfying to cast it that way. Insurers are operating within a system that incentivizes cost containment over recovery, that measures success in financial metrics rather than human outcomes, and operate under a system that has piled so many regulatory requirements onto the claims process that the people doing the work can barely see the people they're supposed to be helping over the mountain of paperwork.

The villain, to the extent there is one, is the system itself — a system that has gradually, almost imperceptibly, shifted its center of gravity away from the injured worker and toward its own institutional needs. The insurance phase of workers' compensation is where that shift is most painfully visible, because it's where the injured worker's expectations of help collide most directly with the system's priorities of efficiency.

Workers' Recovery doesn't ask insurers to stop being prudent with money. It asks them to be prudent with people. It asks them to recognize that the most cost-effective claim is not the one that was denied the fastest or settled the cheapest, but the one where the injured worker was treated with respect, provided with the right care, communicated with honestly, and returned to a functional life in a reasonable time. That's not charity. That's good business. The industry just needs to adjust its spreadsheets to prove it.

In the next chapter, we'll follow our injured worker from the insurance labyrinth into the medical system — where they'll discover that the merry-go-round has more horses, more music, and considerably more nausea than they were expecting.

Chapter 6
The Medical Merry-Go-Round

You've been hurt at work. You've told your supervisor. You've filled out the forms. You've received the letter from the insurance company welcoming you to your new life as "Dear Claimant." Now, finally, mercifully, you get to see a doctor.

Or at least, you get to see a doctor that the system approves of, at a time the system finds convenient, for a duration the system deems appropriate, to receive treatment the system considers medically necessary. Other than that, it's exactly like going to your own doctor.

In the same way that a merry-go-round is exactly like actually going somewhere.

* * *

Whose Doctor Is It, Anyway?

The question of who chooses the treating physician in a workers' compensation claim is one of those delightfully simple questions that the system has managed to make extraordinarily complicated. As with most things in workers' comp, the answer depends on where you live.

In some states, the injured worker gets to choose their doctor. In others, the employer or insurer directs the worker to an approved physician or medical network. In still others, it's some hybrid arrangement where you have free choice but only from a pre-approved list, or you can choose your own doctor but only after the initial visit with the company's doctor, or you can switch doctors but only once, or twice, or only with a written request submitted during a waning crescent moon while Mercury is in retrograde.

The jurisdictional variation here is staggering. There are more than fifty different approaches to physician selection across the United States, and they change with the regularity of seasons. Each state has crafted its own solution to the tension between the worker's right to choose their care and the employer's interest in controlling costs, and each state is absolutely certain that its approach is the correct one.

For the injured worker, the practical effect of all this jurisdictional creativity is confusion. Many workers don't know they have a choice. Many who do know are given the choice in the same way a waiter recites the specials: too quickly, with too little context, at a moment when they're not in a position to make an informed decision. "You can see Dr. Smith at the Occupational Health Clinic, or you can choose your own provider from our approved network. Here's a list of 340 names. You have until Thursday."

And thus begins the medical merry-go-round. The worker grabs a horse, holds on, and hopes it's going somewhere useful.

* * *

The Occupational Health Clinic: Where You're a Number (Again)

For many injured workers, the first medical encounter in the comp system is the occupational health clinic. These are medical facilities that specialize in workplace injuries and are often contracted by employers or insurers as the default first stop for treatment.

Some of them are excellent. Staffed by physicians who understand occupational medicine, who communicate well with both the patient and the employer, and who are genuinely focused on getting the injured worker better and back to work. These clinics exist, and when they're good, they're really good.

And then there are the others.

The injured worker arrives at the clinic. The waiting room is decorated in a style best described as "early DMV." There are plastic chairs. There is a television mounted in the corner showing daytime talk shows at a volume that suggests someone lost the remote in 2014 and hasn't looked for it since. There is a clipboard. There are forms. More forms. Always more forms. The worker has now filled out their injury information so many times that they could describe the mechanism of injury in their sleep, which is unfortunate because the pain medication is making them drowsy and they might actually do that.

The doctor, when they finally appear, spends an average of twelve to fifteen minutes with the patient. In that time, they need to take a history, perform an examination, render a diagnosis, develop a treatment plan, determine work restrictions, fill out the required paperwork, and communicate their findings to the employer and the insurance company. Twelve minutes. For context, that's less time than it takes to order and receive a pizza.

The doctor is not lazy or uncaring. They are operating within a system that pays per visit, which means the economic incentive is to see as many patients as possible in as little time as possible. It's the fee-for-service model at its most counterproductive: a system that rewards speed over thoroughness, volume over outcomes, and efficiency over the one thing the injured worker actually needs — time and attention.

* * *

The Independent Medical Examination (That Isn't Entirely Either)

If there is a single medical procedure in workers' compensation that generates more controversy, more frustration, and more lawyer jokes than any other, it is the Independent Medical Examination, universally known as the IME.

The IME is, in theory, an objective evaluation performed by an independent physician who has no stake in the claim. The purpose is to provide an unbiased medical opinion on the nature and extent of the injury, the appropriateness of the treatment, and the worker's ability to return to work. It's the medical equivalent of a second opinion, ordered by the insurance company to make sure everyone's on the same page.

In practice, the IME is one of the most contentious elements of the entire system, and the word "independent" does a lot of heavy lifting.

The IME doctor is selected and paid by the insurance company. Let's just sit with that for a moment. The entity that is paying for the claim is choosing and compensating the doctor who is supposed to provide an independent opinion about the claim. This is the structural equivalent of letting one team in a baseball game choose the umpire and pay their salary, then insisting with a straight face that the umpire is neutral.

Not all IME doctors are biased. Many are reputable physicians who take the independent part of their title seriously, and call it as they see it regardless of who's paying. But the structural incentive is real, and injured workers know it. The worker shows up to the IME feeling like they're walking into an ambush. They're being examined by a doctor they didn't choose, in an office they've never been to, knowing that this person's opinion could override everything their own treating physician has said. The power dynamic is not subtle.

The true challenge here is that, like every other segment of every other industry in every other corner of the world, bad actors can exist. Very early in my workers' compensation career, I encountered one such actor. It was at a Florida conference where my company was exhibiting, when a doctor who had just relocated to Florida stopped to chat. Now, this man didn't know me from Adam, but that did not dissuade him from sharing his passion for doing IME's. In particular, he loved doing IMEs for one specific carrier, a name you would know but shall not grace these pages, because, in his words, "All I have to do is write whatever they want and they pay me $1200." Now, do I believe that the carrier intentionally found a doctor because he was willing to openly lie? No, not really. What was more likely is they found a doctor who consistently supported their perceptions, beliefs, and their conviction they are right. Despite the possible lack of intent, the result is just as insidious. A scumbag doctor willing to screw injured workers for fun and profit makes a negative impact that can tarnish the reputation of all in that segment of the industry.

The IME itself can be remarkably brief. The examinations that are supposed to determine whether a worker is genuinely disabled or ready to return to work sometimes last less than twenty minutes — a fraction of the time the treating physician has spent with the patient over weeks or months. And yet, the IME doctor's opinion frequently carries more weight in the claims process than the treating physicians. The doctor who has seen the patient once for twenty minutes can overrule the doctor who has treated them for six months. If that seems backwards, that's because it is.

* * *

The Referral Carousel: Now Spinning Faster

One of the more disorienting experiences in workers' compensation medical care is the referral process, which can feel less like a coordinated treatment plan and more like being passed from hand to hand at a very unpleasant party.

Your primary treating physician examines you and determines you need to see a specialist. A referral is made. But the referral needs to be authorized by the insurance company, which triggers a utilization review, which we discussed in the previous chapter. Assuming the referral is approved — and that's not always a safe assumption — you are now scheduled to see the specialist. In three weeks. Because the specialist who accepts workers' compensation patients has a full schedule, partly because workers' comp reimbursement rates may be lower than private insurance and many specialists have decided that treating injured workers simply isn't worth the administrative headache.

Three weeks later, you see the specialist. The specialist examines you, orders additional imaging or tests, and schedules a follow-up. The additional imaging needs its own authorization. Another utilization review. Another wait. The imaging is performed. The results go to the specialist. A follow-up appointment is scheduled. In two more weeks. You are now five to six weeks from your initial referral, and you still don't have a definitive treatment plan.

Each step in this carousel involves its own paperwork, its own authorizations, its own delays, and its own opportunities for something to fall through the cracks. A referral gets lost. An authorization is denied. The specialist's office doesn't have the imaging results. The imaging facility sent the results to the wrong doctor. The insurance company needs the specialist to fill out a form that the specialist's office has never seen before and doesn't know how to complete.

Meanwhile, the injured worker is at home, waiting. Waiting for authorizations. Waiting for appointments. Waiting for results. Waiting for someone, anyone, to tell them what's happening with their body and when they're going to feel better. This is the "Waiting Game" that we'll explore more fully in a later chapter, but it begins right here, in the medical system, where every step in the treatment process seems designed to introduce another delay.

The merry-go-round keeps spinning. The music keeps playing. But nobody seems to be getting anywhere.

* * *

The Prescription Pad and the Elephant in the Room

We cannot discuss medical care in workers' compensation without addressing the issue that has consumed more attention, generated more legislation, and destroyed more lives than perhaps any other medical topic in the system's recent history: opioids.

The opioid crisis did not originate in workers' compensation, but workers' compensation became one of its most fertile breeding grounds. For years, the system's approach to pain management was straightforward: the worker is in pain, prescribe something for the pain. The fact that the "something" was frequently a powerful and highly addictive opioid was treated as a clinical detail rather than a systemic catastrophe in the making.

The result was predictable in hindsight and devastating in practice. Extended claim durations. Higher medical and indemnity costs. Workers who entered the system with a back injury and exited — if they exited at all — with a back injury and an addiction. The medication that was supposed to manage the pain became its own source of suffering, and in the worst cases, its own cause of death. Opioid overdoses have become an increasing share of work-related fatalities, a sentence that should be as shocking to read as it is to write.

To its credit, the industry has begun to respond. States like Washington and California have implemented prescription drug monitoring programs and treatment guidelines that have made meaningful progress. Formulary restrictions, while sometimes frustrating in their rigidity, have reduced inappropriate prescribing. But the underlying problem — a system that reaches for a pharmaceutical solution to a problem that is often as much psychological and social as it is physical — has not been fully addressed. We treat the pain. We don't always treat the person who is in pain. And there is a world of difference between the two.

* * *

Maximum Medical Improvement: The Finish Line Nobody Explains

At some point in the medical journey, the injured worker will encounter a term that sounds clinical, feels final, and is almost never adequately explained to them: Maximum Medical Improvement, or MMI.

We mentioned MMI back in Chapter 3, when we discussed the industry's love affair with unexplained jargon. Here's where it actually matters.

MMI means that the treating physician has determined that the worker's condition has stabilized and is unlikely to improve substantially with further treatment. It does not mean the worker is healed. It does not mean the worker is pain-free. It does not mean the worker is back to where they were before the injury. It means the medical system has done what it can do, and what you've got now is, more or less, what you're going to have.

For the injured worker, MMI can feel like being abandoned at the side of the road. You've been riding this merry-go-round for months, seeing doctors, attending therapy, following treatment plans, waiting for authorizations, enduring IMEs, and filling out forms. And now someone is telling you that the ride is over, and this is as good as it gets. If you're lucky, "as good as it gets" means you're functional and ready to return to a productive life. If you're not lucky, it means you're being handed a permanent impairment rating and pointed toward a settlement negotiation.

The impairment rating itself is another adventure. In most states, it's determined using the AMA Guides to the Evaluation of Permanent Impairment, a publication that has had several incarnations over the last 40 years or so. While it has been criticized in some quarters by those who allege it is based on physician consensus rather than evidence-based medicine, its supporters argue that the updated versions represent the most objective way to analyze and rate impairment. Whether it is the result of a consensus of medical experts or the product of extensive analysis of scientifically supported medicine, The Guides are in many states the definitive book on determining impairment levels. Still, despite the best efforts of very bright experts, there is still a potential misalignment in how they are used. The Guides are designed to measure the impact of impairment on daily living activities, not on work capacity. And yet, in almost every state, the impairment rating is used to calculate permanent disability benefits, which are fundamentally about lost work capacity. We are using a tool designed to measure one thing to calculate something entirely different, and then wonder why the numbers don't feel right to anyone.

* * *

The Doctor Who Doesn't Know You

Here is something fundamental that gets lost in the machinery of workers' compensation medical care: the doctor-patient relationship.

In the regular healthcare world — flawed as it is — you typically have a doctor who knows you. Who has your history. Who has seen you over time and understands you as a whole person, not just a body part with a diagnosis code. That relationship is therapeutic in itself. Trust, familiarity, and continuity of care are not luxuries. They are clinically significant factors in recovery.

In workers' comp, the injured worker is frequently sent to a doctor they've never met, in a clinic they've never visited, to be treated for an injury that exists in the context of a medical history the doctor doesn't have. The treating physician may have no access to the worker's primary care records. They may not know about the pre-existing conditions, the medications, the previous injuries, or the psychological history that could be critical to understanding and treating the current injury. They're treating a chapter without having read the book.

And yet, we expect this doctor — in their twelve-minute visit, with their incomplete information, under the watchful eye of a utilization review process that may second-guess their decisions — to deliver outcomes as good as or better than the regular healthcare system. This is not a reasonable expectation. It is a structural absurdity.

* * *

What Medical Care Under Workers' Recovery Would Look Like

The medical system in workers' compensation isn't broken because doctors are bad. Most of them are dedicated professionals working within constraints that would frustrate a saint. It's broken because the system around them is designed to manage costs rather than optimize healing. Workers' Recovery would reorient the medical experience around a few core principles.

First, select physicians on outcomes, not discounts. We covered this in the previous chapter, but it bears repeating in the medical context. The doctor who gets the worker back to function in six weeks at a higher per-visit cost is cheaper — dramatically cheaper — than the doctor who provides six months of treatment at a discounted rate. Track outcomes by physician and reward the ones who heal. The data already exists; we just need to use it for the right purpose.

That data actually shows, despite the benefits and comfort of using a family physician, that employer directed care can produce superior outcomes, when the right doctors who understand occupational medicine are utilized.

Second, streamline authorizations. The referral carousel we described is not a treatment plan; it's an obstacle course. When a treating physician recommends a specialist, imaging, or a procedure, the default should be approval, not review. This is specifically pertinent when you are employing doctors with proven track records. Let doctors be doctors. Let them practice medicine. Reserve utilization review for outliers and patterns, not routine care decisions. Every authorization delay is a recovery delay, and recovery delays cost everyone more in the long run.

Third, reform the IME process. If the system insists on second opinions — and there are legitimate reasons for them — the process should be genuinely independent. Joint selection of IME physicians, standardized examination protocols, and a requirement that the IME doctor spend a minimum amount of time with the patient would go a long way toward making the process credible to the people it affects most.

Fourth, and most importantly, focus on function. The question that should drive every medical decision in the system is not "what is the diagnosis?" or "what does the impairment rating say?" but "what does this person need to get back to living their life?" Return to function — the ability to pick up a child, walk the dog, bend down and smell the roses — should be the organizing principle of every treatment plan. From that foundation, return to work follows naturally. And it is far more likely to get buy in from the injured worker.

The merry-go-round doesn't have to be the ride. Under Workers' Recovery, medical care would look less like a bureaucratic carousel and more like a straight line — from injury to treatment to healing to function. It's not a radical vision. It's what the system was supposed to be all along.

But before we get to the destination, there's another stretch of the journey that deserves its own chapter — the long, agonizing, soul-testing period between injury and resolution when the injured worker's primary occupation becomes waiting. Waiting for the phone to ring. Waiting for the mail to arrive. Waiting for someone, somewhere, to tell them what comes next.

The Waiting Game. It's longer than you think.

Chapter 7
The Waiting Game

It is 10:14 on a Tuesday morning. You know this because you have looked at the clock eleven times in the last hour. You are sitting on your couch, in the same spot you have occupied for most of the past six weeks, watching a television show you have no interest in because the alternative is staring at the wall, which you have also done, and which is somehow worse.

Your phone is on the cushion next to you. It has not rung. You have checked to make sure it is not on silent. Twice. You have also checked your email, your mailbox, and the tracking status of a package you ordered three days ago because it is the only thing in your life currently progressing toward a resolution.

You are waiting. For a call from your adjuster. For the results of an authorization request. For a specialist appointment that is still two weeks away. For someone to tell you whether you still have a job, whether your treatment will continue, whether your benefits will be extended, and whether the life you had before the injury is something you will ever get back.

Nobody is coming to the door. Nobody is calling. The system has you on hold, and the hold music stopped playing a long time ago.

* * *

The Anatomy of Waiting

Waiting, in the workers' compensation system, is not a bug. It is a feature. Not an intentional one — nobody sat down and designed a system with the explicit goal of making injured workers wait as long as possible — but a feature nonetheless, baked into the architecture of the process so thoroughly that it would require a structural overhaul to remove.

Consider the timeline of a moderately complex claim. The injury occurs. The employer reports it, which may take anywhere from the same day to several days, depending on the jurisdiction's reporting deadline and the employer's enthusiasm for meeting it. The insurer receives the report and assigns an adjuster, which takes a day or two or five, depending on staffing levels. The adjuster reviews the file, contacts the employer, contacts the injured worker — or attempts to — and begins the investigation, which may take one to three weeks. During this period, the worker may or may not be receiving treatment, depending on whether the employer provided immediate medical care or whether everyone is waiting for the claim to be "accepted" before treatment begins.

The claim is accepted — or denied, which triggers its own cascade of waiting as the appeal process lumbers into motion. If accepted, treatment authorizations begin, each with their own review cycle. Specialist referrals are made, each requiring approval and scheduling. Diagnostic imaging is ordered, authorized, performed, interpreted, and reported. Follow-up appointments are scheduled weeks out. And at every step, there is a gap — a space between one action and the next where nothing happens except the passage of time and the accumulation of anxiety.

Add up all those gaps and you get weeks. Sometimes months. Sometimes, in the truly complex or contested claims, years. Years of a person's life spent in a state of suspended animation, waiting for a system that moves at the speed of bureaucracy to decide their fate.

* * *

What Waiting Does to a Person

The medical literature on the psychological effects of uncertainty is extensive, and none of it is encouraging. Prolonged uncertainty activates the same stress responses in the brain as actual threat. The body doesn't distinguish between "I might be attacked by a bear" and "I might lose my benefits next month." The cortisol flows either way. The sleep disruption happens either way. The erosion of mental health happens either way. The bear, at least, has the courtesy to either show up or not. The workers' compensation system keeps you wondering indefinitely.

The injured worker who is stuck in the waiting game experiences a predictable progression. First, there is anxiety — the constant low-grade hum of not knowing what comes next. Then frustration, as the delays mount and the reasons for them remain opaque. Then anger, directed at the adjuster who doesn't call back, the employer who has gone silent, the doctor who can't see them for three weeks, and the system that seems designed to test their patience rather than restore their health. And finally, for some, there is resignation — the quiet surrender of someone who has concluded that nobody is coming, nobody cares, and the path of least resistance is to accept whatever the system eventually offers, even if it's a fraction of what they deserve.

That progression — from anxiety to frustration to anger to resignation — is not a personal failing. It is a rational response to an irrational situation. The system creates the conditions for psychological deterioration and then treats the deterioration as a complication of the injury rather than a consequence of the process.

And here is the part that should alarm everyone with a financial interest in the system: every stage of that progression makes the claim more expensive. Anxious workers perceive more pain. Frustrated workers lose trust in the process and become less cooperative. Angry workers hire attorneys. Resigned workers stop trying to recover and settle into disability. The waiting game doesn't just harm the worker. It harms everyone. The only party that benefits from delay is inertia itself.

* * *

Who Am I Now? (The Identity Crisis Nobody Talks About)

There is a dimension of the waiting game that the system almost entirely ignores, and it may be the most damaging one of all: the loss of identity.

For most people, work is not just a paycheck. It is a central pillar of who they are. It's where they go every day. It's the people they see. It's the routines that structure their time. It's the source of their professional identity, their sense of competence, their feeling of contributing something meaningful to the world. When you ask someone "What do you do?" they don't say "I exist." They name their job. It is, for better or worse, how we define ourselves.

The injured worker who enters the waiting game loses all of that. They are no longer a carpenter, a nurse, a warehouse worker, a teacher. They are a claimant. Their daily routine is no longer structured by work but by medical appointments, phone calls that don't come, and the slow erosion of everything that made them feel useful. They are, in a very real sense, adrift — disconnected from the work that defined them, disconnected from the colleagues who were their daily community, and increasingly disconnected from the person they were before the injury.

This is not melodrama. This is clinical reality. The research on the psychological impact of prolonged work absence is clear: the longer a worker is away from their job, the less likely they are to return. After six months of absence, the probability of ever returning to work drops precipitously. After a year, it approaches zero for many workers. The waiting game isn't just a delay. It is a one-way conveyor belt toward permanent disability, and every week the system adds to the wait is another step in that direction.

Remember the disability mindset we discussed in Chapter 1? This is where it takes root. Not in some inherent laziness or entitlement on the part of the worker, but in a system that strips away their identity, isolates them from their community, leaves them alone with their pain and their anxiety, and then wonders why they're not "motivated to recover."

* * *

The Bills Don't Wait (Even When Everything Else Does)

While the injured worker is waiting for the system to act, the rest of their life is not waiting with them. The mortgage is due. The car payment is due. The electric bill, the grocery bill, the kids' school expenses — none of these have a "pending workers' comp claim" deferral option.

Workers' compensation indemnity benefits replace only a portion of the worker's pre-injury wages — typically two-thirds, subject to a state-imposed maximum. While those payments are generally tax free, that amount doesn't offset losses for lower income workers whose tax obligations are not, as a percentage, a significant portion of their paycheck. And the maximum cap can be quite punishing for higher earners.

Or rather, people who were higher earners, until a workplace injury turned their life upside down.

For workers who were already living paycheck to paycheck, which describes a startling percentage of the American workforce, even the full benefit amount may not cover basic expenses. When benefits are delayed — and they are frequently delayed — the financial stress compounds the physical and psychological stress in ways that are genuinely devastating.

Credit cards get maxed out. Savings, if there were any, evaporate. Families make impossible choices: medication or groceries, rent or physical therapy, keeping the car or keeping the heat on. These are not hypothetical scenarios. These are the daily realities of people trapped in a system that is ostensibly designed to protect them from exactly this kind of hardship.

The financial pressure also creates a perverse incentive that works against recovery. A worker who is desperate for income is more likely to accept a premature settlement — a lump-sum payment that closes the claim but may be far less than the true value of the injury and the future care it requires. The system's delays, in effect, create the financial desperation that drives workers to accept less than they're owed. It is a mechanism for reducing claim costs that nobody designed but everyone benefits from — everyone, that is, except the injured worker whose best option is recovery that may never fully occur.

* * *

The Ripple Effect: Families in the Waiting Room

We talked in Chapter 4 about the Four Points of Communication and the importance of including the injured worker's spouse or partner in the recovery process. Here is where that concept becomes most urgent.

The injured worker does not wait alone. Their family waits with them. The spouse who watches them deteriorate. The children who sense the tension but don't understand it. The household that reorganizes itself around the injury — who does the chores the worker can no longer do, who drives them to appointments, who absorbs the mood swings that come with chronic pain and chronic uncertainty.

The spouse's response to the situation is enormously influential. A supportive, informed partner can be the single greatest asset in a worker's recovery. A frightened, uninformed partner can inadvertently become the greatest obstacle. "Don't go back too early – you'll hurt yourself again." "You should call a lawyer – they're trying to screw us." "You're never going to be the same." These are the cancerous thoughts we discussed in Chapter 4 – and they don't always originate in the worker's own mind. Sometimes they come from the kitchen table, late at night, from a partner who is just as scared and just as uninformed as the worker.

The current system has no mechanism for addressing this. The adjuster doesn't call the spouse. The employer doesn't reach out to the family. The doctor treats the patient, not the household. The family exists in the system's blind spot, invisible and unserved, absorbing the shrapnel of an injury that happened to one person but affects everyone around them.

I once listened to Corey Staver, CEO of David Corey Company, tell a compelling tale that highlights this situation perfectly. His company had been hired to modify a parent's home in order to accommodate their daughter who had suffered extreme brain injury when hit by a car while working. While the medical community had told the family she would need to be in long term care for the rest of her life, the family insisted she be home, and the insurance company agreed to the modifications to make it possible. It was a pandemic era job, and supply issues caused some delays in the construction. Staver flew to New England where the job was located to meet with the injured woman's family. They were all there. Mother, father, siblings, aunts and uncles. It was a good-sized group. He started the meeting by asking them to tell him about their daughter, their sister, their niece. For 45 minutes they talked about her, described who she had been, and what type of person she was. They eventually got down to business, and he assured them they would get the project completed.

As he was leaving, the injured woman's mother stopped him and thanked him for visiting. Then she paused, and sadly said, "This has been an extraordinarily lonely experience."

How could that possibly be? The woman was in a top tier medical facility. She had adjusters, case managers, physicians, specialists, nurses, and more all working to a common goal. Yet the family felt alone. Isolated. Unseen by the system.

Under Workers' Recovery, the family would not be an afterthought. They would be a point of communication. Not because it's nice, but because it works. An informed, supported family produces better recovery outcomes than an isolated, frightened one. The research supports this. Common sense supports this. The only thing that doesn't support this is the current system, which has never thought to ask.

* * *

Enter the Attorney (Stage Left, With a Business Card)

There is a moment in many workers' compensation claims when the waiting game produces a very specific outcome: the injured worker hires an attorney.

This moment is treated by employers and insurers as a turning point — the instant when a "simple claim" becomes a "represented claim" (that's industry jargon for litigated, and yes, the system has jargon for this too). The involvement of an attorney is viewed as an escalation, a sign that the claim is now adversarial, and that costs are about to increase significantly. And they usually do.

But here's the question that the industry rarely pauses to ask: why did the worker hire an attorney in the first place?

Even though it is true in some cases an injured worker has an attorney before the employer knows there was an accident, in the vast majority of claims, that is not the case. The answer to "why" is not greed, fraud, or a predisposition toward litigation. The answer is the waiting game. The worker hired an attorney because nobody was returning their calls. Because they didn't understand the process and nobody explained it. Because their benefits were delayed and nobody told them why. Because they received a denial letter written in a language they couldn't decode and nobody offered to translate. Because they felt abandoned, confused, and powerless, and the attorney's advertisement —

"Injured at work? We can help." — was the first time in weeks that anyone had offered to help them with anything.

The industry spends enormous resources managing litigated claims. It spends relatively little on preventing them. And the prevention is not complicated. Communicate. Return the phone calls. Explain the process. LISTEN. Treat the worker like a person. Most litigated claims are not the result of bad injuries. They are the result of bad experiences. Fix the experience and you fix the litigation rate. But that requires investing in people and communication, which the system has historically preferred to spend on lawyers of its own.

* * *

Breaking the Wait

The waiting game is not inevitable. It is a product of choices — structural choices, staffing choices, process choices, communication choices — and those choices can be made differently.

Workers' Recovery would attack the waiting game from multiple angles. There would be faster claim acceptance decisions, driven by streamlined investigation processes and a presumption of compensability for clearly work-related injuries. Reduced caseloads for Recovery Specialists, so that no injured worker sits by a silent phone wondering if anyone remembers they exist. Pre-authorized treatment pathways would be used for common injury types, eliminating the utilization review delays that stretch a simple referral into a six-week odyssey. And above all, proactive communication — reaching out to the worker before they have to reach out to you.

The research on early intervention is overwhelming and consistent. Claims that are actively managed from day one — with prompt medical treatment, clear communication, and genuine engagement with the injured worker — resolve faster, cost less, produce better outcomes, and generate fewer lawsuits than claims that are left to marinate in the waiting game. With Workers' Recovery, every study, every data set, every analysis would point in the same direction: speed matters, engagement matters, and human connection matters.

The system knows this. The data has been saying this for decades. And yet the waiting game persists, because changing it requires investment, restructuring, and a willingness to measure success in recovered lives rather than managed costs.

In the next chapter, we'll follow our injured worker as they attempt the final leg of the journey: return to work. It should be the triumphant conclusion to a difficult road. Instead, for too many workers, it's one more obstacle course — a "plot twist" that can feel less like a homecoming and more like walking into a room where nobody saved you a seat.

Chapter 8
Return to Work: The Plot Twist

The doctor says you're ready. Or ready enough. The restrictions have been updated, the paperwork has been signed, and someone from HR has called to say you can come back on Monday. Light duty, they say. Modified work. We'll ease you back in.

Monday arrives. You drive to work for the first time in three months. You park in the same spot. You walk through the same door. Everything looks the same.

Nothing feels the same.

The coworker who used to eat lunch with you gives a quick nod and looks away. Your supervisor greets you with the warmth of someone welcoming a contractor they've never met. The desk you're assigned to is not your desk. The work you're given is not your work. You are back in the building, but you are not back.

Welcome to the plot twist.

* * *

The Great Misunderstanding

Return to work is, in theory, the happy ending. The system's success story. The moment when the injured worker has been treated, has recovered sufficiently, and is now resuming their productive role in the workforce. It is the destination toward which every claim is ostensibly navigating.

In practice, return to work is one of the most misunderstood, poorly executed, and emotionally fraught phases of the entire workers' compensation process. And the central misunderstanding is this: too many stakeholders treat return to work as a date on a calendar rather than a process that begins long before the worker walks back through the door.

The employer sees a return-to-work date as the finish line — the day the claim stops costing money and the position gets filled again. The insurer sees it as the day indemnity payments end. The doctor sees it as the day the treatment plan has achieved its clinical objectives. Everyone is looking at return to work from their own vantage point, and from each of those vantage points, the worker's return is a resolution.

The worker sees it differently. For the worker, return to work is the beginning of a new phase of anxiety. Can I do the job? Will it hurt? Will I re-injure myself? Do my coworkers resent me? Does my supervisor trust me? Have I been replaced in every way that matters except on the org chart? The employer sees closure. The worker sees an exam they haven't studied for.

* * *

The Mistrust That Follows You Back

We discussed workplace stigma in Chapter 4 — the Scarlet "C" that marks an injured worker from the moment they file a claim.

That stigma doesn't disappear when the worker returns. In many cases, it intensifies.

There is a persistent, largely unspoken suspicion that accompanies returning workers: are they really better, or are they just back? Supervisors watch more closely. Coworkers note every wince, every accommodation, every task the returning worker can't perform. The worker is simultaneously expected to prove they're healthy enough to be there and forgiven for nothing if they show any sign that they're not.

This creates a no-win situation. If the injured worker performs well, the suspicion shifts to "maybe they weren't that hurt after all." If they struggle, it confirms the suspicion that they came back too soon, or worse, that they're milking the situation. The narrative has been written before they arrived. The returning worker's job is to navigate it without tripping any of the invisible wires.

And the returning worker feels every bit of it. They feel the sideways glances. They sense the conversations that stop when they enter the room. They know, with the certainty that only social exclusion can produce, that they are being evaluated on a different standard than everyone else in the building. This is not paranoia. It is perception, and in the psychology of recovery, perception is reality.

* * *

The Paper Clip Problem (Revisited)

We visited light duty back in Chapter 4, where we observed employers parking injured workers in corners with make-work assignments and training videos on infinite loop. Now that we've walked through the medical merry-go-round and the waiting game, the light duty problem takes on an even darker dimension.

Consider the journey the injured worker has been on. They've been hurt. They've navigated the paperwork. They've been minimized by the system. They've waited by the phone. They've had their identity stripped down to a claim number. They've fought through the medical carousel, endured the IME, survived the financial squeeze. And now, finally, they're back at work. They see a light at the end of the tunnel.

And the light turns out to be a fluorescent bulb in a back office where they've been assigned to sort files nobody needs.

The psychological impact of meaningless work after a long recovery cannot be overstated. The worker has spent weeks or months fighting to get back. Fighting through pain, through bureaucracy, through anxiety and isolation. They have been told, by every chapter of this book's worth of system actors, that the goal is return to work. And now they're here, and the work they've returned to tells them, more clearly than any denial letter ever could, that they are not valued.

Not every employer does this. The good ones — and we cataloged their virtues in Chapter 4 — create light duty assignments that are meaningful, that contribute to the operation, and that make the worker feel like a functional member of the team. But the bad ones? The bad ones turn return to work into a punishment, and then express surprise when the worker doesn't seem particularly grateful to be there.

* * *

Return to Function: The Concept That Changes Everything

We've been building toward this moment for seven chapters. The beating heart of Workers' Recovery. The idea that reframes the entire system. Here it is.

Return to Function.

The traditional system is organized around Return to Work. The goal is to get the worker back on the job. The metrics measure how quickly they return, how many days of indemnity were saved, how much the claim cost compared to projections. It is an employer-centric, cost-centric framework, and it has dominated the industry for decades.

The problem is that Return to Work, as currently practiced, often treats the worker as a means to an end. Get them back. Close the claim. Hit the metric. The worker's experience of returning — whether they're physically ready, emotionally prepared, functionally capable of performing meaningful work — is secondary to the administrative fact of their presence in the building.

Return to Function flips the script. Instead of asking "when can this worker return to their job?" it asks, "what functions does this worker need to restore to return to life?"

Every injured worker wants to pick up their child or grandchild. They want to walk the dog. They want to bend down and smell the roses. They want to sleep through the night without pain waking them up. They want to drive a car, climb stairs, carry groceries, sit through a movie, play catch in the backyard. These are not work functions. These are life functions. And restoring them is what genuine recovery looks like.

When you focus on restoring life functions, something remarkable happens. The worker buys in. They are no longer a passive recipient of a process being done to them. They are an active participant in a recovery that is designed around what matters most to them. They have a goal they can see, feel, and measure — not in impairment ratings or disability percentages, but in the ability to do the things that make life worth living.

And from that foundation, return to work becomes a natural extension rather than an administrative mandate imposed from above. A worker who can pick up their grandchild can probably lift the components at their workstation. A worker who can walk the dog can probably stand for a shift. The functional restoration drives the vocational restoration, and it does so with the worker's full engagement rather than their reluctant compliance.

There is evidence that activity and work can actually lessen perceived pain. This is not wishful thinking. This is research. The worker who returns to meaningful activity — whether at work or in their daily life — often experiences a reduction in pain that no medication could achieve. The body heals better in motion than in stagnation. The mind heals better with purpose than without it. Return to Function harnesses both of these realities.

* * *

Why Return to Work Has a Trust Problem

There is a great deal of mistrust of Return to Work efforts from certain quarters. It is perceived by some as a backhanded attempt to avoid indemnity obligations and save costs overall. And that perception is not entirely without merit.

When the primary motivation behind return to work is cost savings rather than recovery, the worker can tell. They can tell when the light duty assignment is designed to check a box rather than contribute to their healing. They can tell when the urgency to get them back has more to do with the loss run than their lumbar spine. They can tell when "return to work" really means "return to the building so we can stop paying you to stay home."

This mistrust is corrosive. It turns what should be a collaborative process into an adversarial one. The worker resists returning because they believe the employer's motives are financial, not rehabilitative. The employer pushes harder because the costs are mounting. The insurer applies pressure because the reserves are growing. And the attorneys — on both sides — are taking notes.

Return to Function dissolves much of this mistrust, because the goal is transparently in the worker's interest. Nobody argues against the worker being able to pick up their grandchild. Nobody questions the motivation behind restoring the ability to walk the dog. When the framework is built around the worker's own goals, the adversarial dynamic loses its fuel. The worker isn't being pushed back to work for the employer's benefit. They're being supported back to function for their own benefit. And from there, work follows.

* * *

When You Can't Go Back: Training for What's Next

Not every injured worker can return to the job they held before the injury. Some injuries leave permanent impairments that make the previous position impossible. The construction worker who can no longer climb. The nurse who can no longer lift patients. The laborer whose body simply cannot do what it used to do. These are realities that no amount of optimism can wish away.

For these workers, the system's current approach is often woefully inadequate. Vocational rehabilitation, where it exists, is underfunded, inconsistently applied, and frequently treated as an afterthought rather than a core component of the recovery process. Workers who lack the skills for alternative positions are left to navigate the job market on their own, armed with a permanent impairment rating and a resume gap that most employers view with suspicion.

Workers' Recovery must contain a meaningful training and educational component. People left with permanent impairments after an injury may not be able to return to the position they once held, and they may lack the skills for other available positions. We as an industry must be better at providing assistance to accommodate both an impairment and the development of new skill sets. This is not charity. It is the logical extension of a system that claims to serve injured workers. If the system is responsible for the worker's recovery, that responsibility doesn't end when the medical bills stop. It ends when the worker has a viable path to a productive life.

A worker who receives meaningful retraining and transitions to a new career is a success story. A worker who is handed an impairment rating and abandoned to figure it out is a failure of the system, regardless of how neatly the claim file was closed.

* * *

What a Successful Return Actually Looks Like

We've spent most of this chapter on what goes wrong. Let's spend a moment on what goes right, because it does go right sometimes, and when it does, the results are proof that Workers' Recovery isn't a theory. It's a practice that works wherever it's genuinely tried.

A successful return to work starts long before the return date. It starts with communication — the employer staying in touch throughout the recovery, the worker knowing their job is waiting, the supervisor planning a meaningful role that fits within the medical restrictions. It starts with the Four Points of Communication keeping everyone informed and aligned. It starts with a Recovery Specialist who has the time and training to coordinate the transition rather than just scheduling it.

On the day of return, the worker is welcomed; not processed but welcomed. The supervisor has a conversation, not a checklist. The coworkers have been briefed and encouraged to be supportive. The assignment is ready and it's real work – modified as needed, but genuine and contributory. The worker feels, from the first moment, that they are a member of the team who has been missed and whose return matters.

In the days and weeks that follow, the transition is monitored. The restrictions are respected. The worker's feedback is sought and valued. As they progress, their duties expand naturally, guided by their functional capabilities rather than arbitrary timelines. The goal is not to rush them to full duty. The goal is to build a sustainable return that doesn't result in re-injury, relapse, or the quiet resignation of a worker who has concluded that being back isn't worth the effort.

This isn't utopian fantasy. Companies do this every day. And the outcomes are measurably, consistently, dramatically better than the alternative. Outcomes include lower re-injury rates, shorter claim durations, higher employee retention, and better morale. Not to mention, they have workers who speak well of the company that took care of them – which, in the age of employer review sites and social media, is worth more than any insurance premium discount.

* * *

Return to work doesn't have to be a plot twist. It can be the resolution the story was building toward all along. But only if we stop treating it as a calendar date and start treating it as what it really is: the final, critical phase of a recovery that has to be earned, supported, and sustained.

We've now walked the full length of the injured worker's journey, from the moment of injury through the paperwork, the employer response, the insurance labyrinth, the medical merry-go-round, the waiting game, and the return to work. It's been funny in places and infuriating in others. But behind every joke and every critique, there's been a single, consistent argument: the people in this system deserve better.

In the next chapter, we're going to stop laughing for a moment. Because the human cost of getting this wrong — the emotional devastation, the financial ruin, the broken relationships, and the lost lives — deserves to be spoken about plainly, without humor, and without flinching.

Chapter 9
The Human Cost Nobody Talks About

This chapter is different.

For the past eight chapters, we've employed some lighthearted and subtle humor as a lens — a way to examine the absurdities, the failures, and the frustrations of a system that affects millions of lives. Any jokes were intentional. They were strategic. They were designed to keep you reading about things that might otherwise make you turn away.

This chapter has no jokes. Because what happens to people when the system fails them is not funny. It has never been funny. And it deserves to be spoken about in plain language, without the cushion of comedy, so that the weight of it can be felt by anyone who has the power to change it.

* * *

The Injury Behind the Injury

Every workplace injury produces two wounds. The first is the one that shows up on the medical report — the torn rotator cuff, the herniated disc, the fractured wrist, the chemical burn. It has a diagnosis code, a treatment protocol, and a projected recovery timeline. The system knows how to deal with this wound. Imperfectly, as we've seen, but it knows.

The second wound is the one that doesn't appear on any form. It is the psychological, emotional, and social damage that accompanies the physical injury and, in many cases, far outlasts it. It is the depression that settles in during the third week of sitting on the couch. The anxiety that builds with every unanswered phone call. The shame of needing help with things you used to do without thinking. The grief — and it is grief — for the person you were before the injury and may never be again.

The system barely acknowledges this second wound. There is no box on the First Report of Injury for "emotional devastation." There is no treatment authorization code for "loss of identity." The adjuster's file does not track the number of nights the injured worker lay awake at 3 a.m., staring at the ceiling, wondering if this is what the rest of their life looks like. These things are real. They are measurable. They affect recovery outcomes as profoundly as any physical complication. And the system treats them as though they don't exist.

* * *

The Darkness That Moves In

Depression is not a side effect of workplace injury. It is a predictable, well-documented, and frequently inevitable consequence of it. Studies consistently show that injured workers experience depression at rates far exceeding the general population. The combination of chronic pain, financial stress, social isolation, loss of routine, and loss of identity creates conditions in which depression doesn't just appear — it thrives.

And depression, once it arrives, changes everything about the claim. It increases the perception of pain. It decreases motivation. It impairs decision-making. It extends disability duration. It makes the worker less likely to engage with treatment, less likely to pursue return-to-work opportunities, and more likely to develop chronic pain syndromes that persist long after the original injury has healed. Depression is not a complication of the injury. It is a complication of the system — a system that creates the perfect environment for it and then offers almost nothing to treat it.

Mental health is present as a co-morbid condition in more than twenty percent of cases where the primary cause of absence is a physical injury. One in five, and that number almost certainly understates the reality, because many injured workers never report their psychological symptoms, either because they don't recognize them, because they're afraid of the stigma, or because they've learned from experience that the system doesn't want to hear about it.

In many jurisdictions, mental health conditions that arise from a physical injury face additional barriers to compensability. The worker must prove that the psychological condition is causally related to the work injury, which requires documentation, specialist evaluation, and often litigation — none of which are easy for a person who is already struggling to get out of bed in the morning. The system that created the conditions for depression then makes the treatment of that depression contingent on the worker's ability to navigate the very bureaucratic maze that contributed to it. It is a closed loop of institutional failure.

* * *

The Relationships That Break

A workplace injury does not happen to one person. It happens to a family.

We explored this in Chapter 7 when we discussed the family's experience in the waiting room. But the waiting room is just the beginning. The long-term impact of a serious workplace injury on relationships is profound, pervasive, and almost entirely invisible to the system that set it in motion.

Marriages strain and sometimes break. The injured worker who was once a provider becomes a dependent. The partner who was an equal becomes a caregiver. Roles that were established over years are upended in a moment, and the recalibration is painful for both sides. The injured worker feels guilty, diminished, and angry — not at their partner, but at themselves for not being who they used to be. The partner feels exhausted, resentful, and guilty for feeling resentful. Neither knows how to talk about it, because the system has given them no language, no resources, and no support for what they're going through.

Children are affected in ways that may not be visible for years. The parent who can't play catch anymore. The household tension that children absorb even when they don't understand it. The birthday party the family can't afford because the benefits check was late. The move to a smaller apartment because the mortgage became unsustainable. These are not abstract consequences. They are lived experiences, happening in real homes, to real families, because a system designed to help injured workers has failed to account for the fact that injured workers do not exist in isolation.

Remember the mother who told Corey Staver, "This has been an extraordinarily lonely experience." She was not talking about loneliness in the sense of having no one around. She was surrounded by medical professionals, claims managers, and case workers. She was talking about the loneliness of being unseen — of having a family's anguish treated as peripheral to a process that was technically about her daughter but functionally about paperwork, procedures, and payments.

* * *

The Financial Wreckage

We touched on the financial pressure in Chapter 7. Here, we need to look at the full scope of what happens when a serious injury meets a system that moves slowly.

Workers' compensation benefits are designed to be a safety net, not a replacement for income. Two-thirds of pre-injury wages, tax free but subject to a cap, is the standard formula in most states. For a worker earning $50,000 a year, that translates to roughly $33,000; sometimes with no adjustment for the additional costs that often accompany an injury. These might be unreimbursed transportation to medical appointments, child care, medications not fully covered by the workers' comp pharmacy benefit, denied assistive devices and home modifications. Even simple lawn maintenance and house cleaning, along with the hundred small expenses that accumulate when your body can no longer do what it used to.

For workers at the lower end of the income scale – a space many injured workers inhabit, because the occupations with the highest injury rates are also among the lowest-paid – the math is simply impossible. The benefits don't cover the bills. Savings are depleted within weeks. Debt accumulates. Credit is destroyed. The financial damage from a serious workplace injury can take years or even decades to recover from, long after the physical injury has healed.

And for those who end up permanently disabled, the picture is bleaker still. Permanent disability benefits vary wildly by state, and in many jurisdictions they are inadequate by any reasonable measure. A worker who loses the full use of their dominant hand may receive a lump-sum payment that sounds significant until you divide it by the forty years of earning capacity it's supposed to replace. The Grand Bargain promised security. For too many permanently disabled workers, it delivers a check that doesn't come close.

* * *

The Quiet Epidemic

We addressed the opioid crisis in Chapter 6. Here, we need to reckon with its human toll.

For every statistic about opioid prescribing rates and formulary reforms, there is a person. A person who was given medication for legitimate pain, who took it as prescribed, and who discovered, weeks or months later, that they could no longer function without it. A person who entered the workers' compensation system with a back injury and exited with an addiction that would define the rest of their life — assuming it didn't end it.

Substance abuse among injured workers is not limited to opioids. Alcohol abuse rises sharply during prolonged disability. The combination of chronic pain, isolation, depression, and financial stress creates a perfect incubator for dependency. The worker who starts having a drink to take the edge off the pain at night becomes the worker who needs several drinks to sleep. The transition from coping mechanism to dependency is gradual, invisible, and devastating.

The system has begun to address the prescription side of this equation, and progress has been made. But the broader reality — that the system's own dysfunction drives people toward substances as a way of surviving it — remains largely unexamined. We treat the addiction when we find it. We do almost nothing to prevent the conditions that create it.

* * *

The Ones We Lose

There is a statistic that the workers' compensation industry does not track, because it falls outside the boundaries of what the system considers its responsibility. It is the number of injured workers who take their own lives.

Research in this area is limited, but what exists is sobering. Studies in multiple countries have found that workers with occupational injuries are at significantly elevated risk of suicide compared to the general population. The combination of chronic pain, depression, financial distress, social isolation, and loss of identity — every factor we've discussed in this chapter — creates a risk profile that clinicians recognize immediately.

The system does not cause these deaths. But the system's failures contribute to the conditions that make them more likely. Every unanswered phone call. Every unnecessary delay. Every denial that left a worker feeling abandoned. Every week of isolation that could have been prevented with a single act of communication. None of these things, individually, drive a person to the edge. But cumulatively, over months and years, they can erode the psychological resources that keep a person holding on.

This is not written to assign blame. It is written to assign urgency. If the human cost of the system's dysfunction includes even one preventable death, that should be enough to demand change. The evidence suggests the number is far higher than one.

* * *

Why This Chapter Matters

This book has argued, through light humor (hopefully) and analysis, that the workers' compensation system needs reform. That argument is built on data, on industry experience, on the logic of better outcomes and lower costs. Those arguments are valid and they are important.

But this chapter exists because the most important argument for reform is not financial. It is moral.

Every delay that could be eliminated is a week of suffering that didn't have to happen. Every denial issued without adequate review is a person left without care they needed. Every adjuster too overloaded to return a phone call is a worker sinking deeper into isolation. Every family left in the dark is a household under stress that could have been eased with a single conversation. Every worker assigned to count paper clips is a human being whose dignity has been weighed against a cost metric and found less important.

The people who work within this system are not callous. They are, in the overwhelming majority, dedicated professionals who care deeply about the people they serve. The failure is not one of compassion. It is one of architecture. The system was not designed with the human cost in mind. It was designed around process, compliance, and cost management. The human cost is what happens in the spaces between the procedures — in the gaps, the silences, the waits, and the forms that ask about everything except how the person is actually doing.

Workers' Recovery is, at its core, an argument that those spaces matter. That the human cost is not a side effect of the system but a measure of the system. That we should judge workers' compensation not by how efficiently it processes claims but by how effectively it restores lives.

Seven thousand people will be injured at work today. Each one of them is someone's parent, child, spouse, or friend. Each one of them woke up this morning expecting a normal day. Each one of them deserves a system that sees them as a person first and a claim number second.

They deserve better than this. And we can do better than this.

In the next chapter, we'll lay out what "better" looks like — a comprehensive vision for Workers' Recovery that takes everything we've discussed and translates it into a roadmap for change. We will try to restore a bit of humor, because the work ahead requires energy, not grief. But the weight of this chapter should travel with us. It is the reason the rest of the book exists.

Chapter 10
A Better Way

So. We've toured the wreckage.

We've watched an injured worker navigate the paperwork avalanche, endure the employer shuffle, survive the insurance labyrinth, ride the medical merry-go-round, and wait — and wait, and wait — for a system that was supposed to help them. We've laughed at the absurdities, flinched at the failures, and in the last chapter, sat with the human cost of getting this wrong.

Now it's time to build something better.

Workers' Recovery is not a wish list. It is not a theoretical exercise. It is a practical, achievable framework for transforming workers' compensation from a system that manages claims into a system that restores lives. Every proposal in this chapter has been discussed somewhere earlier in this book. What follows is the blueprint — all of the pieces, assembled in one place, for anyone ready to pick up a hammer.

* * *

It Starts With a Word

We begin where we began: with the name.

Workers' Compensation becomes Workers' Recovery. Not as a rebranding exercise. Not as a marketing campaign. As a foundational shift in what the system tells everyone — workers, employers, insurers, physicians, legislators — that it is here to do. Compensation says: we will pay you for your trouble. Recovery says: we will help you get better. The word sets the expectation. The expectation drives the behavior. The behavior determines the outcome.

And the naming convention extends throughout the system. Claims adjusters become Recovery Specialists. Claims Departments become Recovery Management Divisions. Injured workers become recovering workers. These are not cosmetic changes. They are cognitive reframings that, as the research we discussed in Chapter 1 demonstrates, have measurable effects on how people think, communicate, and act. The folks in subrogation will need to find new titles, but they're resourceful people. They'll manage.

* * *

Recovery Specialists: Trained, Equipped, and Given a Fighting Chance

The transformation of the claims adjuster into a Recovery Specialist is not accomplished by changing a title on a business card. It requires three structural changes that the industry has resisted for decades: better training, lower caseloads, and different metrics.

Training first. The fact that nearly half of the industry's organizations lack a formal training program for new employees responsible for managing claims is not a statistic. It is a scandal. Recovery Specialists must be trained not only in the technical and regulatory aspects of their work but in communication, empathy, recovery-oriented case management, and the psychological dimensions of injury and disability. They need to understand that their phone calls are clinical interventions. That their words shape recovery trajectories. That the way they communicate a denial or explain a process can be the difference between a worker who engages with recovery and a worker who hires a lawyer. This is not optional professional development. It is core competency.

Caseloads second. A Recovery Specialist with 250 or more active files cannot be successful. Period. The math does not work, as we demonstrated in Chapter 5 with the 1.92-minutes-per-claim calculation. Meaningful caseload reduction is not cheap, and it requires hiring more staff. But the cost of an additional Recovery Specialist is dwarfed by the cost of the claims that spiral out of control because the existing ones are too overloaded to intervene. The most expensive adjuster is still the cheap one with 250 files on their desk.

Metrics third. Recovery Specialists should be measured on return-to-function outcomes, not on how quickly they close files or how much they save on reserves. When the metric is cost containment, every decision bends toward cost. When the metric is recovery, every decision bends toward the worker. This isn't idealism. It's incentive design. People optimize for what they're measured on. If we want recovery, we have to measure recovery.

* * *

The Four Points of Communication

The traditional three points of contact — adjuster, employer, medical provider — becomes the Four Points of Communication. The differences are not just in the number.

First, the word "contact" becomes "communication." Contact is a voicemail. Communication is a conversation. The current system allows a message left on an answering machine to satisfy the requirement. Under Workers' Recovery, actual two-way communication is the standard. If you haven't spoken to the person, you haven't communicated.

Second, the fourth point: the worker's spouse, partner, or primary support person. We've made the case for this in Chapters 4, 7, and 9. The family is not peripheral to recovery. The family is central to it. An informed, supported family produces better outcomes. A frightened, invisible family produces worse ones. Including them is not an intrusion. It is a clinical necessity.

Third, communication must be proactive, not reactive. The system currently waits for the worker to call — and then doesn't answer. Under Workers' Recovery, the Recovery Specialist reaches out first. Before the worker has to wonder. Before the anxiety builds. Before the cancerous thoughts take root. The phone call that prevents a problem is infinitely cheaper than the litigation that results from the silence.

* * *

Return to Function Before Return to Work

We laid out the case for Return to Function in Chapter 8, and it remains the beating heart of Workers' Recovery. The concept is straightforward: before asking what the worker can do for the employer, ask what the worker needs to do for themselves.

Every recovery plan under Workers' Recovery would begin with a simple, powerful question: what functions would you most like to restore? Not "describe your disability." Not "rate your pain on a scale of one to ten." What do you want to be able to do again? Pick up your grandchild. Walk the dog. Drive a car. Sleep through the night. These goals become the architecture of the treatment plan, the benchmarks for progress, and the motivational fuel that keeps the worker engaged in their own recovery.

Return to Work becomes a natural extension of Return to Function, not a separate mandate imposed from above. The worker who can pick up their grandchild can probably handle the physical demands of their workstation. The functional restoration drives the vocational restoration, and it does so with the worker's buy-in rather than their resistance. This is the key that the current system misses: recovery works best when the person recovering is invested in the goal. And people invest in goals that matter to them, not goals that matter to someone else's spreadsheet.

* * *

Medical Care That Heals

The medical reforms under Workers' Recovery are driven by a single principle: select physicians on outcomes, not discounts.

The data to do this already exists. Insurers track treatment durations, medical costs, and return-to-work dates for every claim. The problem is that this data is used to identify expensive claims rather than effective doctors. Workers' Recovery flips the lens. Physicians who consistently return workers to function quickly and without re-injury are preferred and rewarded, even at a higher per-visit cost. Physicians whose patients languish in treatment without demonstrable progress are identified and, if the pattern persists, removed from the network. This is a fee-for-outcome model within the existing fee-for-service structure, and it is entirely achievable with current technology.

Utilization review must be reformed from a cost-control gatekeeping function into a genuine quality assurance mechanism. When a treating physician with a proven track record recommends treatment, the default should be approval, not review. Reserve the scrutiny for outliers. Let the good doctors practice medicine without having to justify every imaging order to a reviewer who has never met the patient.

The IME process needs structural independence. Joint selection of examining physicians, standardized protocols, and minimum examination times would move the process from its current adversarial posture toward something that both sides can trust. An IME that is genuinely independent serves everyone's interests, including those of the insurers.

* * *

Employers as Recovery Partners

The employer's role under Workers' Recovery transforms from passive reporter to active recovery partner. This requires investment in three areas: training, communication, and meaningful return-to-work programs.

Supervisor training must go beyond compliance checklists and cost containment messaging. Supervisors need to understand that the first five minutes after an injury report are the most important clinical intervention in the entire claim. They need the language and the confidence to respond with genuine concern, to communicate clearly about what happens next, and to maintain a relationship with the injured worker throughout recovery. This is not a seminar. It is a skill set that requires practice, reinforcement, and organizational commitment.

Communication must be continuous, not episodic. The employer who goes silent after the claim is filed is creating the conditions for litigation. The employer who stays in touch — even when there's nothing new to report, even when the worker has an attorney, even when the conversation is uncomfortable — is investing in an outcome that is better for everyone. And as we discussed, the fact that a worker has retained counsel does not mean the employer must stop communicating. It means the particulars of the case require the attorney's involvement. But asking how someone is feeling, sharing workplace news, and expressing genuine care? That never needs to stop.

Return-to-work programs must be built around dignity and contribution, not paper clips and training videos on repeat. This translates to meaningful light duty and real work that contributes to the operation. It includes a transition plan that respects medical restrictions while restoring the worker's sense of being valued. Every person needs to have value. The employer who provides it will see better outcomes than the one who parks the worker in a corner and hopes they quit.

* * *

Paperwork That Serves People, Not the Other Way Around

The documentation infrastructure of workers' compensation is overdue for a renovation that would make even the most ambitious home remodeler flinch.

The renovation should start with a standardized First Report of Injury that works across all jurisdictions. The technology exists. The data standards exist. The logic of that concept must overcome the territorial protectionism and ego that has prevented it thus far. The 3,700 jurisdictional forms currently in circulation are a monument to fragmentation, not to diligence. It is time to build the common FROI that the industry has been discussing for decades.

We must use plain language on every form. Remember Dave, our injured warehouse worker from chapter 3? If he cannot read and understand a form without a translator, that is a failure. Dave is not the problem. The form is.

We should streamline the process to accommodate one-time data entry where the worker tells their story once. The system captures it, with no more Rashomon effect. The telling of the same story seven times to seven different people, continually reinforcing the pain narrative and the identity of disability, would be a thing of the past.

And the design would focus on recovery-oriented intake. This would create forms that ask not only "what is wrong?" but "what would you most like to restore?" The first question documents a problem. The second establishes a goal. Both are necessary. Only one points toward recovery.

* * *

Legislate for Outcome, Not Process

State legislators and regulators play a critical role in the Workers' Recovery framework, and it is a role that requires a fundamental shift in approach.

Too often, legislative reform in workers' compensation concentrates on process rather than outcomes. The result, time and again, is additional layers of bureaucratic procedure, confusion, and delay. We create new reporting requirements, new compliance standards, and, of course, new forms, because no reform is complete without new forms. Each reform, individually, may be well-intentioned. Collectively, they add sediment to the geological formation of bureaucracy that our injured friend Dave is already struggling to climb.

Examples of legislative folly abound in workers' compensation, but I can think of no better example than the Colorado "Notice to Employer of Injury" poster. It is a required workplace poster known as Form WC-50, mandated under the Workers' Compensation Act. To say the legal printing and posting requirements are fairly specific would be an understatement. In 2022, the Colorado Legislature passed House Bill 22-1363, which made several changes to the states workers' compensation system. It changed the employee reporting period from 4 days to 10 days, updated the employee-notice language, required a new employer notice/poster, and added tolling provisions if the employer fails to provide the notice.

The posting notice, Form WC-50, was not only mandated by the legislation to contain specific language, the typeface, or lettering, was required by law to be at least ½ an inch high. That combination resulted in the mandated designing of a poster so large Dave could read it from his office on the moon. It is literally a movie poster size creation. It is so ridiculously large I suspect workers were injured in the state just trying to hang the damn thing. Or, I suppose, when building the wall to hang it on. It does serve, however, as a great example of how misguided legislation is developed without thought or concern for outcomes or practicality.

Instead, Workers' Recovery asks legislators to define clear, measurable end goals and craft legislation toward those goals. What does success look like? Shorter disability durations. Higher return-to-function rates. Lower litigation rates. Better worker satisfaction. These are outcomes that can be measured, tracked, and legislated toward. The process for achieving them should be left, as much as possible, to the professionals doing the work — with accountability for results rather than compliance with procedures.

Workers' Recovery must not exist for the bureaucrats. It must exist for the 7,000 people who get hurt at work every day. If a regulation doesn't serve their recovery, it needs to justify its existence — or get out of the way.

* * *

The Business Case (Because Someone Will Ask)

Chapter 9 made the moral argument. This section makes the financial one. Not because the financial argument is more important, but because any proposal that requires investment will eventually face someone with a spreadsheet and a skeptical expression.

The business case for Workers' Recovery is built on a simple premise: the current system's failures are expensive. Litigation driven by poor communication costs more than simple and direct effective communication. Extended disability driven by delayed treatment costs more than prompt treatment would have. Permanent disability driven by the waiting game costs more than early intervention would have. Turnover driven by poor return-to-work experiences costs more than meaningful light duty would have. At every failure point we've identified, the cost of doing nothing exceeds the cost of doing better.

The companies that already practice elements of Workers' Recovery — the ones we described in Chapter 4 as "what the good ones get right" — demonstrate this consistently. They have lower claim costs, facilitated by shorter injury durations. There are fewer litigated claims. Overall they have higher retention and achieve better outcomes; for both their injured workers and their bottom line. These are not anomalies. They are the predictable results of treating injured workers as people rather than as line items.

Workers' Recovery is not a cost center. It is a cost strategy. It just happens to also be the right thing to do — which, in a system built on the Grand Bargain, should not be treated as a coincidence.

* * *

Version 2.0, Not a Demolition

Workers' Recovery is not a repudiation of workers' compensation. It is an upgrade. Same foundational principles. Same Great Compromise. Same recognition that workers who are injured on the job deserve care and support. But refocused, restructured, and reoriented around the outcome that should have been at the center all along: helping people get better.

None of the proposals in this chapter are impossible. Some of them are already being practiced by forward-thinking employers, insurers, and jurisdictions. The challenge is not invention. It is adoption. It is moving from pockets of excellence to system-wide commitment. It is overcoming the institutional inertia of a system that has been doing things a certain way for over a century and finds change uncomfortable.

But the alternative to change is the status quo. And the status quo, as we've spent nine chapters documenting, is a system that processes claims adequately and serves people inadequately. A system that manages costs while losing people. A system where the claimant is no longer relevant to the process.

That's not good enough. Not for the 7,000 who will get hurt today. Not for the families who will wait by the phone. Not for the workers who deserve to pick up their grandchild, walk the dog, and bend down and smell the roses.

Yet there is one more critical component to successful Workers' Recovery. A component so essential to the achievement of positive outcomes that it deserves its own dedicated chapter. That critical piece is the injured worker and their state of mind. Their perception, their viewpoint, their ultimate acceptance of the process, it's not just important; it is required for any level of positive result. We will delve into how a Workers' Recovery system would help guide that worker to a positive result in the next chapter.

Chapter 11
The Injured Worker's Responsibility to the Injured Worker

We've spent ten chapters talking about what the system owes the injured worker. Better communication. Better training. Better medical care. Better processes. A system redesigned around recovery rather than paperwork. All of that is true, and all of it is necessary.

But there is a conversation that this book would be dishonest to avoid. A conversation that some will find uncomfortable, and that others will misread as blaming the victim. It is neither. It is a recognition of something that every clinician, every experienced adjuster, and every injured worker who has successfully recovered already knows:

No system, however well designed, can recover for you. The most important person in the recovery process is the person recovering.

* * *

The Most Important Person in the Room

The injured worker is not a passenger in their recovery. They are the driver. Every other participant in the process — the employer, the insurer, the physician, the Recovery Specialist, the family — is support crew. They can provide the vehicle, fuel it, maintain it, and map the route. But the worker is the one behind the wheel. And if the driver doesn't want to go anywhere, the best vehicle in the world will sit in the driveway.

This is not criticism. It is a clinical reality. The research on recovery outcomes across every domain of medicine and rehabilitation points to the same conclusion: patient engagement is the single strongest predictor of successful outcomes. Stronger than the quality of the physician. Stronger than the treatment protocol. Stronger than the speed of the claims process. A worker who is mentally engaged in their recovery, who believes recovery is possible, and who is willing to do the hard, often painful work of getting better will outperform the system's projections almost every time.

A worker who has decided, consciously or unconsciously, that recovery is not possible — that they are permanently broken, that the system is against them, that nothing they do will make a difference, that they are "disabled" beyond repair — will underperform those projections with equal consistency. Not because they are lazy. Not because they are fraudulent. But because the mind and body are not separate systems. What the mind believes, the body follows. A worker who believes they cannot recover is, in a very real neurological sense, correct — because the belief itself becomes the barrier.

* * *

Mindset: The Variable Nobody Measures

The workers' compensation system tracks everything about an injured worker except the thing that matters most: what they think is going to happen.

The file contains the diagnosis, the treatment plan, the work restrictions, the impairment rating, the wage calculation, and roughly forty-seven forms documenting the same event from different angles. What it does not contain is any meaningful assessment of the worker's psychological readiness for recovery. Do they believe they will get better? Do they understand what recovery looks like? Are they frightened, angry, resigned, or hopeful? Are the people around them supporting their recovery or reinforcing their disability? These questions are not soft. They are among the hardest predictors of outcome that the research has identified. And the system ignores them almost entirely.

A worker's mindset on entering the system is shaped by everything we've discussed in this book. The employer's initial response. The adjuster's first phone call. The experience in the waiting room. The language on the forms. The denial letter. The silence. Every interaction either builds the psychological foundation for recovery or erodes it. By the time the worker is sitting on their couch at 10:14 on a Tuesday morning, staring at a phone that doesn't ring, their mindset has been shaped by dozens of system inputs — most of them negative.

This is precisely why the system reforms we outlined in Chapter 10 matter so much. A well-designed Workers' Recovery system doesn't just process claims more efficiently. It actively steers newly injured workers toward positive outcomes by shaping the inputs that form their mindset. Compassionate first response. Clear communication. Prompt treatment. Genuine engagement. Recovery-oriented language. Every one of these interventions is, at its core, a mindset intervention — a deliberate effort to build the psychological conditions in which recovery can succeed.

But even the best-designed system can only create the conditions. The worker has to walk through the door.

* * *

Impairment Is Not Disability

There is a distinction at the heart of this chapter that the workers' compensation system has never adequately made, and that many injured workers have never been taught. It is the distinction between impairment and disability.

Impairment is the physical reality of an injury. It is what the body can and cannot do after the damage has been done and the healing has progressed as far as it will go. A shoulder that no longer rotates fully. A back that can no longer bear heavy loads. A hand that has lost grip strength. These are objective, measurable, medical facts. They are what they are. They do not negotiate.

Impairment is the physical reality, while disability is how the injured worker chooses to deal with it.

That sentence will strike some readers as harsh. It is not meant to be. It is meant to be liberating. Because if disability were simply the inevitable consequence of impairment — if a 15 percent impairment rating automatically meant a 15 percent reduction in the quality of your life — then there would be nothing anyone could do about it. The rating would be the sentence, and the worker would serve it.

But that is not how it works. The world is full of people with significant physical impairments who live full, productive, meaningful lives. People who have adapted, accommodated, and redefined what "normal" looks like for them. People who refused to let what they lost define what they still have. They are not superhuman. They are not in denial. They are people who, at some point in their journey, made a decision — conscious or gradual — that their impairment would be a fact of their life, not the defining fact.

There is Warren, a double above the knee amputee, who shortly after his accident made the focused decision to not let the injury define him. He decided he was "going to be the man I was." And he is. A lifelong adventurer and mountain climber, he has since scaled some of the most challenging peaks in the world. And today, he spends time leading young people with impairment on climbs summiting Mt. Kilimanjaro. His goal is to show them that there is life beyond injury, and their impairment does not define who they are.

There is Bonnie, an author and economist in the Obama administration. She is also a Paralympic Silver and Bronze medal winner in downhill skiing. Bonnie has one leg, having lost the other to a medical condition at the age of four. She credits her mother and others with creating a "vision of success" that told her she could be much more than just a "one-legged African American girl from San Diego." And she is. She is indeed.

And we have Erik, an amputee who lost a leg in a forklift accident. Erik's story represents the quintessential tale outlined earlier in this book; a system saturated with delay and seemingly intent on proving the adage that insanity is doing the same thing over and over and expecting different results. Erik actively fought for a better outcome. He lost over 100 pounds. He wrestled to replace a prosthetic leg that simply did not work yet was repeatedly sent to the same clinic for continually useless refits. Finally, after much wrangling, he forced the system to send him to a different prosthetics maker who provided the proper solution. And today Erik is employed by that prosthetics firm, working with new amputees, helping them adjust to their new life and reality.

I've had the pleasure of meeting these people and others like them. They are all people with distinct impairments, yet we would struggle to define them as disabled. Whether conscious or not, they all made the decision that their physical condition would not define who they were, or the lives they would lead.

And the world is equally full of people with relatively minor impairments who have been consumed by disability. Who have organized their entire identity around what they can no longer do. Who have accepted the system's language of limitation and made it their own. These are not bad people. They are people who were never given the tools, the support, or the framework to make a different choice. The system told them they were disabled. They believed it.

Words mean things. We said that in Chapter 1. Here is where it matters most.

* * *

The Hardest Step: Acceptance

For workers with permanent impairments, there is a moment in the recovery journey that no form prepares them for, and no adjuster is trained to help them navigate. It is the moment of acceptance — the moment when the worker confronts the reality that they are not going to return to the person they were before the injury.

This is not the same as giving up. It is the opposite of giving up. Acceptance is the precondition for genuine recovery. As long as the worker is fighting to restore what cannot be restored — mourning the shoulder that will never rotate fully, raging against the back that will never bear heavy loads — they are oriented toward loss. Their energy is consumed by what is gone rather than invested in what is possible. Acceptance redirects that energy. It says: this is where I am now. This is what I have to work with. Recovery starts from here.

This is profoundly difficult. It requires grieving, which takes time. It requires support, which the current system does not provide. And it requires honesty — from the physicians who must communicate prognosis clearly, from the Recovery Specialists who must guide expectations, and from the worker themselves, who must be willing to hear what they may not want to hear.

The current system is catastrophically bad at this. The MMI designation, as we discussed in Chapter 6, often arrives as an administrative surprise rather than a guided transition. The worker is told their condition has "stabilized" — a clinical word that tells them nothing about how to live with what's left. No one sits them down and says: here is what this means for your life. Here is what you can still do. Here is how other people in your situation have adapted. Here are resources, support groups, training programs, and people who have walked this road before you.

Bethany Hamilton is a professional surfer who at the age of thirteen lost an arm in a shark attack and is the subject of the movie Soul Surfer. She describes her encounter with their family doctor as she came out of surgery after the attack. He informed her that her arm was gone. Then he said, "I am going to give you a list of things you can no longer do. It will be very, very short." He continued with, "Then I am going to give you a list of things you can still do. You just may need to change the way you do them. It will be much, much, longer." That doctor was gold. From the outset he started preparing this young woman for a life that may have changed but was by no means over. Most injured workers simply do not get that important guidance.

Instead, they get a rating and a check. And they are left to figure out acceptance on their own, in the silence that follows the system's departure from their life.

* * *

Guiding, Not Judging

Here is the critical point, and the one that separates Workers' Recovery from the voices that simply tell injured workers to "tough it out" or "get over it": the worker's mindset is not solely the worker's responsibility. It is a shared responsibility between the worker and the system that serves them.

An integral part of Workers' Recovery is understanding that the worker's psychological journey is not a side effect to be managed. It is a core dimension of recovery to be actively supported. The system must help guide the injured worker toward understanding and acceptance — not through platitudes or motivational posters, but through structured, evidence-based interventions that address the psychological reality of injury and impairment.

This means Recovery Specialists trained to recognize when a worker's mindset is becoming a barrier to recovery — and trained to respond with support rather than suspicion. It means physicians who are equipped to discuss prognosis honestly and compassionately, and who understand that delivering a permanent impairment rating is a clinical conversation, not an administrative one. It means access to psychological support, peer mentoring programs, and vocational counseling as standard components of the recovery plan, not afterthoughts triggered only when the claim goes sideways.

It means a system that says to the injured worker: we understand that this is hard. We understand that accepting a new reality is painful. We are here to help you through it, not to judge you for struggling with it. But we also need you to engage. We need you to be an active participant in your recovery, not a passive recipient of benefits. Because the best system in the world cannot recover for you. That part is yours.

* * *

Recovery as Partnership

The title of this chapter is deliberate. It is not "The Injured Worker's Responsibility to the Employer" or "The Injured Worker's Responsibility to the System." It is "The Injured Worker's Responsibility to the Injured Worker."

The obligation is not to the insurance company's bottom line. It is not to the employer's experience modification rate. It is not to the state's disability statistics. The obligation is to yourself. To the person you still are and the person you can still become. To the grandchild you want to pick up. To the dog that still needs walking. To the roses that still need smelling.

Workers' Recovery is, at its fullest expression, a partnership. The system commits to treating the worker as a person, not a claim number. The employer commits to communication, support, and dignity. The insurer commits to prompt, fair, recovery-oriented claims management. The physician commits to outcome-based care. And the worker commits to engaging with their recovery, confronting the realities of their injury, and doing the hard work of getting better.

None of these commitments works in isolation. A worker cannot be expected to engage with a system that ignores them. A system cannot produce results for a worker who has disengaged. The partnership is the point. And when it works — when every stakeholder is oriented toward recovery and the worker is at the center of a system that genuinely supports them — the outcomes are not just better. They are transformative.

Impairment is a fact. Disability is a choice — not a simple one, not an easy one, and not one that anyone should have to make alone. But a choice, nonetheless. And the system's highest calling is to make the better choice possible.

* * *

We've now laid out the full vision of Workers' Recovery — the system's responsibilities and the worker's role within it. But the world is not standing still. In the next chapter, we'll look at the technologies that are coming for this industry — artificial intelligence, automation, data analytics, and more — and ask whether these tools will be used to build Workers' Recovery or simply to make the current system faster and more efficient at doing the wrong things.

Chapter 12
Rise of the Machines: AI and the Future of Workers' Recovery

In a not-too-distant future — and by "not-too-distant" I mean approximately next Tuesday — an injured worker will file a claim and have it acknowledged, investigated, accepted, and assigned to a Recovery Specialist before they've finished icing their knee. An algorithm will have analyzed the injury type, cross-referenced it against millions of similar claims, predicted the optimal treatment pathway, identified the highest-performing physician in the network, and generated a personalized recovery timeline. All before a human being has touched the file.

The question is not whether this is coming. It is already here, in various stages of arrival. The question is whether we're going to use it wisely.

* * *

The Robots Are Coming (And They Don't Need Coffee Breaks)

Artificial intelligence, machine learning, robotic process automation, predictive analytics, natural language processing, wearable technology, telemedicine, blockchain — the parade of technologies marching toward the workers' compensation industry is long, noisy, and shows no signs of slowing down for anyone who isn't ready.

For an industry that took decades to move from paper files to electronic ones — and that still hasn't fully accomplished that transition, as anyone who has visited certain state agencies can attest — the pace of technological change is somewhere between exhilarating and terrifying. Workers' compensation has historically adopted new technology with the enthusiasm of a cat being given a bath. It gets there eventually, but not without a great deal of resistance, noise, and the occasional scratch.

But ready or not, the technology is coming. And it brings both extraordinary promise and significant danger, depending entirely on how the industry chooses to use it.

* * *

The Promise: Faster, Smarter, More Human

The potential benefits of AI and advanced technology in workers' compensation are genuinely exciting, and they align remarkably well with the Workers' Recovery framework.

Consider the waiting game. We spent an entire chapter on the devastating effects of delay. Now imagine a system where AI triages incoming claims in minutes rather than days. Where predictive models identify high-risk claims at intake — not six months later when the claim has already spiraled — and flag them for immediate, intensive human intervention. Where pre-authorized treatment pathways for common injury types are activated automatically, eliminating the utilization review delays that stretch a routine referral into a six-week odyssey. The waiting game doesn't have to end. But it can be dramatically shortened.

Consider the adjuster's caseload. We demonstrated that a Recovery Specialist with 250 files has 1.92 minutes per claim per day. Now imagine AI handling the routine administrative tasks – the documentation, the compliance checks, the status updates, the scheduling – that currently consume the majority of the adjuster's time. If technology can take over even half of the administrative burden, it effectively doubles the time available for what matters most: talking to injured workers. The Recovery Specialist of the future may still have 250 files, but they might have the functional equivalent of a 125-file caseload in terms of available human interaction time.

Consider physician selection. We argued for selecting doctors on outcomes rather than discounts. AI makes this not just possible but routine. Machine learning algorithms can analyze treatment patterns, recovery timelines, re-injury rates, and patient satisfaction data across millions of claims to identify which physicians consistently produce the best outcomes for specific injury types. The doctor who gets back-injury patients back to function faster than anyone else in the network can be identified, preferred, and rewarded – automatically.

Consider communication. Chatbots and AI-powered communication tools can provide injured workers with instant answers to routine questions at three in the morning, when the anxiety is worst and no human is available. They can send proactive check-in messages, track worker sentiment, flag signs of disengagement, and alert the Recovery Specialist when human intervention is needed. Technology cannot replace the human connection that Workers' Recovery demands. But it can ensure that the human connection is deployed where it matters most, rather than consumed by tasks a machine could handle.

* * *

The Danger: Faster at Doing the Wrong Things

Here is where it gets complicated. Because every one of those promising applications has a dark mirror — a version that uses the same technology to make the current system's worst tendencies more efficient.

AI that triages claims can also be used to identify which claims are most likely to be denied successfully. Predictive models that flag high-risk claims for intervention can also flag them for aggressive cost containment. Algorithms that analyze physician data can be used not to find the best doctors but to find the cheapest ones. Automated communication tools can replace human connection rather than supplement it, turning the phone tree we mocked in Chapter 5 into a chatbot that is equally unhelpful but harder to escape.

The technology is agnostic. It does not care whether it is optimizing for recovery or for cost containment. It will optimize for whatever it is told to optimize for, with a speed and efficiency that would make the most determined human cost-cutter look like an amateur. If the system's metrics remain focused on cost — and if AI is deployed to pursue those metrics — the result will not be Workers' Recovery. It will be the current system on steroids:

faster denials, more efficient gatekeeping, more sophisticated ways to avoid paying for the care that injured workers need.

This is not a hypothetical concern. It is already happening. AI-powered utilization review systems are being deployed to speed up denial decisions. Predictive models are being used to identify claims with litigation potential — not to intervene early and prevent the litigation, but to transfer the claim to a specialized defense team. The technology is being adopted by the current system to do the current system's work faster, not to do different work.

And there is a subtler danger still: the same technology that allows us to communicate more rapidly and concisely than ever also runs the risk of further distancing us from the people we are intended to serve. The app that is designed to provide claim information. The chatbot that can competently answer questions. The automated text message that checks in on the worker's progress. The AI-powered voice system that schedules medical appointments. The portal that requires the injured worker to upload their own documents, navigate their own treatment authorizations, track their own deadlines. Each one is faster, cheaper, and more efficient than a phone call from a human being. And each one sends the same quiet message: you are not important enough for a person.

This matters because injured workers notice. They notice when they're asked to rate their pain level on an automated scale but no one asks how they're actually doing. They notice when the system confirms receipt of their medical records but no one confirms whether anyone actually read them. They notice the difference between "your claim has been updated" and "I reviewed your file and here's what happens next." Technology can transmit information. It cannot transmit care.

We have spent this entire book arguing that communication is the single most powerful tool in the recovery process — and that the system's greatest failure is its inability to make injured workers feel heard. Technology that replaces human communication with digital efficiency doesn't solve that failure. It scales it. The injured worker sitting on their couch at 10:14 on a Tuesday morning doesn't need a push notification. They need a voice on the other end of the line that knows their name and asks how they're doing. No app has ever replaced that. None ever will.

* * *

The Human in the Loop

There is a principle in AI ethics called "human in the loop" — the idea that automated systems should always include meaningful human oversight, particularly when the decisions being made affect people's lives. In workers' compensation, this principle is not just ethically important. It is absolutely essential.

An algorithm can predict, with impressive accuracy, the likely duration and cost of a claim based on historical data. What it cannot do is understand why this particular worker is not recovering as expected. It cannot hear the tremor in a voice that suggests depression. It cannot sense the family tension that is reinforcing disability. It cannot recognize that the worker's reluctance to return to work has nothing to do with their physical condition and everything to do with a supervisor who made them feel unwelcome the last time they tried.

These are human insights. They require human perception, human empathy, and human judgment. And they are precisely the insights that determine whether a claim resolves in eight weeks or eighteen months. Technology that frees up the Recovery Specialist's time to have these conversations is invaluable. Technology that replaces those conversations is catastrophic.

The rule must be simple: AI handles the process. Humans handle the people. Any deployment of technology that reduces human-to-human contact in the workers' compensation system is moving in the wrong direction, regardless of how much money it saves. The phone tree in Chapter 5 was already a lesson in what happens when a system prioritizes institutional efficiency over human connection. An AI-powered version of that phone tree would be the same mistake, only smarter and harder to argue with.

* * *

The Injuries We Haven't Met Yet

Technology isn't just changing how we manage injuries. It is changing the injuries themselves.

The nature of work is transforming at a pace that the workers' compensation system has not begun to keep up with. The gig economy has created millions of workers whose employment status is ambiguous and whose access to workers' compensation is uncertain. Remote work has blurred the boundaries between workplace and home, creating jurisdictional puzzles that would give a workers' comp attorney a migraine. Automation is eliminating some physically dangerous jobs while creating new categories of injury — repetitive stress from human-robot collaboration, psychological strain from AI-monitored workplaces, ergonomic injuries from workstation configurations that nobody evaluated because the worker set them up on their kitchen table.

The mental health dimension is growing rapidly. Workers in AI-monitored environments report higher levels of stress, anxiety, and burnout. The psychological impact of working alongside robots — including the existential anxiety of wondering if your job will be next to be automated — is a new category of occupational stress that the current system has no framework for addressing. The injuries of the future may be less about broken bones and more about broken spirits, and the system needs to be ready for both.

Workers' Recovery, with its emphasis on the whole person rather than just the physical injury, is better positioned to address these emerging challenges than the current system. A framework that already accounts for psychological wellbeing, family impact, and return to function doesn't need to be reinvented to address the injuries of the future. It just needs to be implemented for the injuries of today.

* * *

Wearables, Sensors, and the Surveillance Question

Wearable technology and workplace sensors offer tantalizing possibilities for injury prevention. Devices that monitor body mechanics and alert workers when they're lifting improperly. Sensors that detect fatigue patterns and suggest rest breaks before injuries occur. Environmental monitors that identify hazardous conditions in real time. The technology exists to prevent a meaningful percentage of workplace injuries before they happen.

It also exists to create a surveillance environment that would make George Orwell's stomach turn.

Workers who are monitored constantly — their movements tracked, their biometrics recorded, their productivity measured in real time — report higher levels of stress and lower levels of job satisfaction. The same device that could prevent a back injury by alerting the worker to bad lifting form could also be used to discipline the worker for not meeting movement quotas. The line between injury prevention and performance surveillance is thin, and the workers' compensation industry's track record of prioritizing cost containment over worker wellbeing does not inspire confidence that it will always use the technology properly.

Under Workers' Recovery, wearable technology and workplace sensors would be deployed under a clear principle: these tools exist to protect the worker, not to monitor the employee. Data collected for injury prevention purposes must be used for injury prevention purposes — and nothing else. This requires explicit policies, transparent implementation, and genuine worker input into how the technology is deployed. It also requires the industry to resist the very strong temptation to use safety data for cost containment, which is approximately as likely as asking a cat to resist an open can of tuna. But the principle must be established, even if the enforcement will be an ongoing battle.

* * *

A Technology Checklist for Workers' Recovery

For any technology being considered for deployment in the workers' compensation system, the following questions should be asked — and answered honestly:

Does this technology increase or decrease human-to-human contact between the injured worker and the people managing their recovery? If it decreases contact, proceed with extreme caution.

Is this technology being deployed to improve recovery outcomes or to reduce costs? If the honest answer is costs, it may still be worth doing — but it is not Workers' Recovery.

Does this technology serve the injured worker or the institution? If it makes the insurer's job easier but the worker's experience worse, it is moving in the wrong direction.

Does this technology treat the injured worker as a person or as a data point? Algorithms are only as humane as the objectives they're given. If the objective is cost containment, the algorithm will optimize for cost containment, and the worker will be reduced to a number more efficiently than any human system could accomplish.

The machines are rising. They will transform workers' compensation whether the industry is ready or not. The only choice is whether they will be programmed for recovery or for the same old game with faster processors.

* * *

We've now covered the full landscape — the system's failures, the human cost, the reform framework, the worker's role, and the technological future. What remains is the most important chapter of all: what you, the reader, can actually do about it. Whether you're an employer, an insurer, a legislator, a regulator, a physician, an injured worker, or simply someone who believes the system can be better, the next chapter is your call to arms.

The machines can help. But the change starts with people. It always has.

Chapter 13
A Call to Arms

You've read the book. You've toured the system. You've laughed at the absurdities, winced at the failures, and sat with the human cost. You've seen the blueprint for Workers' Recovery and the technologies that could accelerate or undermine it. You've heard the argument, from every angle, that the system can be better.

Now what?

This chapter is for everyone who read this book and thought, "Someone should do something about this." You are someone. And this is the something.

* * *

To the Employers

We have talked a great deal in this book about getting better results for injured workers. Here is a secret we haven't fully disclosed. Better outcomes for injured workers also mean better outcomes for you. You are in business to earn a profit. We get that. You have to look at the numbers, to be sure. However, you also need to make sure you are looking at the right numbers. Better communication, along with prompt, effective, and compassionate care, mean shorter injury durations and less litigation. That translates to less operational disruption and – dare we say it – better outcomes for you. Workers' Recovery provides profitable outcomes for employers.

And you are the first responders of Workers' Recovery. Not in a metaphorical sense. Literally. You are the first people the injured worker sees, the first voice they hear, the first signal they receive about how this is going to go. And as we established in Chapter 4, those first five minutes are the most important clinical intervention in the entire claim.

Here is what you can do, starting tomorrow:

Train your supervisors. Not with a compliance video and a quiz. Train them to be human beings in a moment of crisis. Give them the words. Give them the confidence. Make them understand that "Are you okay?" is not just a kind thing to say – it is the most cost-effective intervention available in the entire workers' compensation system. Practice it. Role-play it. Make it muscle memory. The supervisor who responds with genuine concern in the first five minutes is worth more than every cost-containment strategy your risk department has ever devised.

Stay in touch. When an employee is injured and out on a claim, do not go silent. Call them. Not once – regularly. Ask how they're doing. Share news from the workplace. Tell them their job is waiting, if it is. Tell them they are missed, if they are. And if an attorney has entered the picture, do not let that silence you. You can still communicate. You can still care. The attorney represents the worker's legal interests. You represent the fact that they still belong somewhere.

Build meaningful light duty. If you are assigning injured workers to count paper clips or watch training videos on repeat, stop. Today. Create assignments that contribute to the operation, that use the worker's skills within their restrictions, and that make them feel like a valued member of the team. If you can't think of meaningful work for a returning employee, ask them (or their co-workers). They will have ideas. They have been sitting at home for weeks thinking about exactly this.

Eliminate the stigma. Examine your safety incentive programs and ask whether they are inadvertently punishing injury reporting. Look at your culture honestly and ask whether injured workers are treated as members of the team or as problems to be managed. Remember the ladder. If the injury happened at home, you'd send flowers. The injury happened at work. Respond accordingly.

* * *

To the Insurers

You are the engine room of this system. What you measure, the system optimizes for. What you incentivize, the system produces. And right now, the system is optimizing for cost containment and producing exactly what you'd expect: contained costs and uncontained human suffering.

Here is what you can do:

Invest in your people. The 47 percent of organizations without formal training programs for new claims staff — fix that. Not with a webinar series. With genuine, comprehensive training that includes communication skills, psychological awareness, and recovery-oriented case management alongside the technical fundamentals. Your adjusters — your Recovery Specialists — are the human face of your organization at the most critical moment in the business relationship. Invest in them the way you would invest in any front-line professional whose performance determines your outcomes. Because it does.

Reduce caseloads. Yes, it costs more to hire additional staff. No, it does not cost more than the claims that spiral into litigation because nobody had time to return a phone call. Do the math. Not the short-term math that looks at headcount expense. The long-term math that looks at claim outcomes, litigation rates, duration, and total cost of risk. The most expensive adjuster is the cheap one with 300 files. You know this. Act on it.

Change what you measure. If your Recovery Specialists are evaluated on closure rates and reserve accuracy, they will close files and manage reserves. If they are evaluated on return-to-function outcomes, worker satisfaction, and recovery timelines, they will pursue recovery. Incentive design is not complicated. It just requires the courage to measure what matters rather than what's easy to count.

Select physicians on outcomes. The data is in your systems already. Use it to identify the doctors who heal, not just the doctors who discount. Build networks around performance, not price. A physician who returns workers to function at a higher per-visit cost but in half the time is your most valuable partner. Treat them that way.

And for the love of everything decent, rewrite the denial letter. If an injured worker needs a law degree to understand your correspondence, the correspondence has failed. Plain language. Human tone. Sense of compassion. Clear explanation of what happens next. This is not a regulatory constraint. This is a choice. Make a better one.

* * *

To the Legislators

You hold the pen. You pass the laws. And with respect, some of the laws you've created are part of the problem.

Every time you add a new reporting requirement, a new compliance standard, or a new form, ask yourself: does this serve the injured worker's recovery, or does it serve the bureaucracy's need for documentation? If it's the latter, have the courage to leave it on the drafting room floor. The system already has 3,700 jurisdictional forms. It does not need 3,701.

Legislate for outcomes, not process. Define what success looks like — shorter disability durations, higher return-to-function rates, lower litigation rates, better worker satisfaction — and hold the system accountable for achieving those outcomes. Let the professionals who do the work determine the best process for getting there. Your job is to set the destination, not to mandate the route. And please, for the sake of Dave's wall space, consider the practical implications of your poster requirements.

Standardize where it matters. A national First Report of Injury is long overdue. Plain-language requirements for all worker-facing communications should be mandated, not suggested. The technology and the data standards exist to make these things happen. What has been lacking is the political will to overcome jurisdictional territoriality. Workers do not care which state has the best form. They care about getting better.

And examine the barriers to mental health treatment within the workers' compensation system. If the system's own delays and dysfunction contribute to depression — and they do — then the system has a responsibility to address the depression it helped create. Making it harder for injured workers to access psychological care is not cost containment. It is cost shifting — to the worker, to their family, and to the broader healthcare system.

And there is one more thing. It may be the most important action you can take. And it is a simple one. Legislate a name change for your workers' compensation system. Name it Workers' Recovery. In many, if not most, US jurisdictions, the name of the system is legislatively defined to be workers' compensation. If you want to make a dramatic impact, letting your constituents know there's a new system in town, officially renaming the system and the agency that regulates it will have more initial influence than any other action recommended here, and it will pave the way for the other important changes that are required for this remodel.

* * *

To the Regulators

If legislators set the destination, you build the road. And in many states, you are the ones who determine whether that road leads to recovery or to another layer of bureaucratic compliance.

Your influence on the workers' compensation system is enormous and often underappreciated. You write the rules that translate legislation into practice. You develop the fee schedules that determine what care costs and who provides it. You establish the treatment guidelines that shape medical decision-making. You create the penalty structures that determine whether denying a worker appropriate treatment carries consequences or is simply a cost of doing business. In many ways, legislators set the ceiling. You determine the floor.

The best regulators are already doing Workers' Recovery work, whether they call it that or not. Tennessee's REWARD program — providing resources and training for employers to build genuine Employee Recovery programs — is exactly the kind of initiative that transforms policy language into workplace reality. Physician certification programs that help employers and insurers identify doctors who treat toward recovery rather than simply toward MMI are regulatory innovations with direct, measurable impact on outcomes. These programs exist because regulators saw a gap between what the law intended and what the system was delivering, and built something to close it.

We need more of this. Everywhere.

You are the ones who uncover employers operating outside the system entirely — the ones who deny any benefits at all to injured employees and hope nobody notices. You are the ones who can mandate education on best practices, not as optional continuing education but as a condition of participation. You are the ones with the data to identify which parts of the system are working and which are failing, and the authority to act on what the data reveals.

Workers' Recovery needs regulators who see themselves not as enforcers of compliance but as architects of outcomes. The rules you write, the programs you develop, the standards you set, and the accountability you demand are the mechanisms that turn legislative intent into lived reality for injured workers. Without you, Workers' Recovery is a concept on paper. With you, it is a system that works.

* * *

To the Physicians

You are, in many ways, the most trusted voice in the injured worker's life. The employer may be suspect. The insurer may be adversarial. The attorney may have an agenda. But the doctor — the doctor is the one the worker believes. What you say, how you say it, and when you say it shapes the worker's expectations, their mindset, and their recovery trajectory more than any other single factor.

Use that trust wisely. Set realistic expectations from the first visit. Explain what recovery looks like — not just clinically, but functionally. Tell them what they will be able to do, not just what is wrong with them. Be the doctor who gives the short list and the long list, like the physician who treated Bethany Hamilton. That conversation takes five minutes. Its impact lasts a lifetime.

Communicate with the other stakeholders. The treating physician who operates in isolation — who treats the patient without talking to the employer about restrictions, without coordinating with the Recovery Specialist about the return-to-work plan, without understanding the worker's actual job demands — is practicing medicine in a vacuum. Workers' Recovery requires the physician to be a member of the recovery team, not a solo practitioner handing down edicts from the examining room.

And when the time comes to deliver the news about permanent impairment, do not delegate that conversation to a form. Sit with the worker. Explain what it means. Explain what it does not mean. Help them see the road forward, not just the road that's closed. You may be the only person in the entire system who has the credibility to help them take the hardest step — acceptance — and from that step, genuine recovery begins.

* * *

To the Injured Workers

This book has been, in large part, a case made on your behalf. The system owes you better. The employers, insurers, physicians, and legislators who shape your experience have work to do. That is true, and you have every right to demand it.

But as we discussed in Chapter 11, the most important person in your recovery is you. And there are things that only you can do.

Engage with your recovery. Show up to appointments. Do the exercises. Follow the treatment plan. Ask questions when you don't understand something. Call your Recovery Specialist back. Communicate honestly about how you're feeling — physically and emotionally. The system is imperfect, sometimes maddeningly so, but disengaging from it does not punish the system. It punishes you.

Resist the narrative of permanent limitation. Your impairment is real. Your pain is real. Nobody is asking you to pretend otherwise. But as we demonstrated earlier, disability is not the inevitable consequence of impairment. We cannot emphasize this point enough. *Impairment does not mean disability*. Disability is instead a response to impairment, and you have more control over that response than the system has led you to believe. Seek out the stories of people who have faced similar injuries and built lives beyond them. Warren, Bonnie, Erik — they are not exceptions. They are examples of what is possible when the person recovering decides to be the driver, not the passenger.

Include your family. Don't shut out the people who love you. They are scared too, and they deserve to be informed, included, and supported. Your recovery affects them, and theirs affects yours. The kitchen table conversations matter. Make sure the information driving those conversations is accurate, not anxious.

And if the system fails you — if the phone calls aren't returned, if the denials don't make sense, if the process feels adversarial — speak up. Advocate for yourself. You are not a claim number. You are a person with rights, with value, and with a voice. Use it.

* * *

To the Industry as a Whole

Workers' compensation is an industry of good people operating in a flawed system. The overwhelming majority of the professionals I have met in my years in this field care deeply about the people they serve. They did not enter this profession to deny claims, delay treatment, or make injured workers feel like numbers. They entered it because they believed in the promise of the Great Compromise: that workers who are injured on the job deserve care, support, and a path back to productive life.

That promise is still worth keeping. But it requires all of us to be honest about where the system has drifted from it.

The shift from Workers' Compensation to Workers' Recovery is not a revolution. It is a recalibration. Same foundation. Same principles. Different focus. Different metrics. Different outcomes. It asks every stakeholder to do what they already know is right but what the system has not incentivized them to do: put the recovering worker at the center of every decision.

The changes outlined in this book are not impossible. Many of them are already being practiced by organizations that have decided, on their own, to do better. The challenge is scale. The challenge is moving from pockets of excellence to industry-wide commitment. The challenge is overcoming the inertia of a century-old system that has been doing things a certain way for so long that the way itself has become the purpose.

The system is not the purpose. The people are the purpose. They always were.

* * *

The 7,000

Seven thousand Americans will be injured at work today. By the time you finish reading this sentence, one of them has just gotten hurt. They are in a warehouse, on a construction site, in a hospital, at a restaurant, in an office, on a factory floor. They are someone's parent, someone's child, someone's partner, someone's friend.

In a few minutes, a supervisor will be notified. A form will be produced. A claim will be filed. A file will be opened. And a system will engage that will either help this person recover or process them into a number.

Which one it will be depends on the choices we make. All of us. Employers, insurers, legislators, regulators, physicians, the workers themselves. Every stakeholder in this system has the power to make it better, one decision, one conversation, one phone call at a time.

Workers' Recovery is not a destination. It is a direction. It is the decision to stop managing claims and start restoring lives. To stop counting costs and start counting recoveries. To stop putting people on hold and start putting them first.

Thank you for holding. Your injury is important to us. Now let's prove it.

Epilogue
Still Standing

I came to this industry by accident. Not the workplace kind, thankfully, but the career kind — the sort of unexpected turn that lands you in a field you never studied, never planned for, and couldn't have imagined would become your life's work.

I stayed because of the people.

Not the system. The system, as this book has spent considerable energy documenting, is a Rube Goldberg machine of extraordinary complexity and frequently baffling design. I have spent years inside it, sometimes admiring its ambition, often questioning its priorities, and occasionally wondering whether anyone remembers what it was originally built to do.

But the people. The people are something else entirely.

* * *

I have met adjusters who stayed late to return one more phone call because they knew the person on the other end needed to hear a human voice before the end of the day. I have met employers who drove to an injured worker's home with groceries because they heard the family was struggling. I have met physicians who spent an extra twenty minutes with a patient — uncompensated, unscheduled — because the conversation about acceptance couldn't be rushed. I have met regulators who genuinely agonized over getting it right, even when the political pressures pushed them toward getting it expedient.

And I have met injured workers who humbled me. People who faced injuries that would have broken most of us and chose, through some combination of stubbornness, grace, and sheer refusal to be defined by what happened to them, to build lives that were not just functional but full. Warren on his mountain. Bonnie on her ski slope. Erik in his new career, helping others navigate the road he'd already walked. The mother in New England, waiting in the loneliest room in the system, still fighting for her daughter. These are not abstractions. These are people I have known, and they are the reason this book exists.

* * *

I wrote this book because I believe the system can be better. Not perfect — no system involving human beings, bureaucratic structures, and competing financial interests will ever be perfect. But better. Meaningfully, measurably, life-changingly better.

I used humor because I've learned, over years of trying, that people are more willing to examine uncomfortable truths when they're laughing than when they're being lectured. A joke can open a door that a policy paper can't. Once you're laughing at the absurdity of a system that puts people on hold while telling them their call is important, you've already conceded the point. The laughter is the concession. The reform is the follow-through.

But underneath the humor, there has always been a simple conviction: that the word "recovery" is better than the word "compensation." That the person behind the claim number deserves to be treated as a person. That communication is not a soft skill but a clinical intervention. That impairment does not have to mean disability. That the system's highest purpose is not to manage risk but to restore lives.

These are not radical ideas. They are, when you strip away the bureaucracy and the inertia and the century of accumulated procedure, obvious ones. The kind of ideas that make people nod and say, "Of course. Why aren't we already doing that?"

That question — why aren't we already doing that? — is the one I hope this book leaves with you. Not as an accusation, but as an invitation. The answer is not that the people in the system don't care. They do. The answer is that the system itself has drifted, slowly and almost imperceptibly, away from the people it was built to serve. Correcting that drift is not a revolution. It is a recalibration. And it starts with anyone who decides to make one decision differently tomorrow than they made it today.

Somewhere right now, a worker is getting hurt. Maybe it's a fall. Maybe it's a repetitive strain that finally became too much. Maybe it's a piece of equipment that had other ideas about their continued physical integrity. Whatever it is, their life just changed, and they don't fully know it yet.

In a few minutes, someone will hand them a clipboard. Someone will ask them to describe the mechanism of injury. Someone will open a file with their name on it — or, more likely, a number.

What happens after that is up to us. *Let's make it a recovery.*

Acknowledgments

There are some important acknowledgements I would like to make here. I would like to thank Abbie Hudgens for her editing skill, as well as her commitment to a better workers' compensation industry. Abbie was the person responsible for shepherding through significant reforms for her state of Tennessee, vastly improving the situation for both employers and their injured workers in the state. She is and will always be an influential force in workers' compensation, and her willingness to write the foreword for this book as well as provide valuable editing insight is greatly appreciated.

I would also be remiss if I did not acknowledge WorkCompCollege.com, as well as the hundreds of professionals who have supported it in a quest to create a better workers' compensation system than the one they currently toil in. While I am a founding member of WorkCompCollege.com, it is the skill and commitment of these people who have collectively created an educational system that is focused on training professionals for workers' compensation 2.0 – the system we are calling Workers' Recovery.

And finally, there are the thousands of injured workers whose stories helped create the Workers' Recovery concept.

Back in 2000, when we first launched WorkersCompensation.com, one of the features of the site that proved extremely popular was our open discussion center. While available for all to use, it was dominated by injured workers. There were professionals that participated, helping those that they could, but by and large the biggest population of that discussion board consisted of those injured on the job. Some were angry workers long trapped in a system that had fundamentally failed them. Some were people who had gone through a workplace injury, and while no longer in the system found themselves tied to a community where their shared experiences helped others. And there were the confused and befuddled, stumbling into a world previously unknown and completely lost in the process.

Over the years that discussion board collected thousands of threads, and hundreds of thousands of posts. It was, beyond a shadow of a doubt, the best education one could find regarding how workers' view the system, and where its glaring shortcomings existed.

Over all those years, one thing remained consistent. Newly injured workers, on their first venture into that little community, would enter long and detailed posts about their injury, the immediate aftermath, and the confusion in their lives it had brought. But, almost without exception, they would end their post by asking a variant of the same question.

How much will I be paid?

How much will I make?

How big will my settlement be?

It did not take long to figure out they, through complete ignorance of the system, were asking the wrong question. They should have been asking, "How can I get better?" "How can I make sure I receive the best care?" "How can I get back to health and function?"

It was with that simple observation that I began to realize that workers' compensation was completely misbranded. These injured workers entered our system completely oblivious as to what it was, how it operates, and what it pays. But they did understand the word compensation, and that is where they routinely focused. For the vast majority that wasn't out of greed; it was simply the one thing they understood in a vast sea of bewilderment.

These workers, and the stories they told, are the reason that the Workers' Recovery model was born. It was their willingness to share their frustration and concerns that led to the formation of this concept. Unfortunately, that discussion forum no longer exists, having been taken down shortly after I left the company. It is a loss, as the information we could glean from it was invaluable. I cannot go back to the board and thank the legions of injured who helped me conceptualize workers' compensation 2.0, but I can certainly do so here.

Thanks to all those workers' for sharing their stories. I, and possibly many people in the future who achieve better outcomes through a compassionate system that communicates well, will owe you a great debt.

About the Author

Bob Wilson is a founding partner and president of Workers' Compensation Educational Services, LLC, which provides a variety of education and information services for the workers' compensation industry. These include the platforms WorkCompCollege.com, WorkersCOMPliance.com. WorkCompEvent.com, and Judicial Survey.com. He is the founder and former President & CEO of WorkersCompensation.com, a position he held for 23 years.

He is an experienced presenter for the workers' compensation industry and is the author of "From Bob's Cluttered Desk", a blog repeatedly named as a top workers' compensation blog by LexisNexis. Additionally, he has been named one of the "50 Most Influential People in Workers' Comp" by the SEAK National Workers' Compensation and Occupational Medicine Conference and is the recipient of a Comp Laude Industry Leader Award as well as a 2025 Culture Shaper Award. Known for an extraordinary sense of humor, his presentations reflect both entertaining and practical advice for both people managing claims as well as the people "picking up the tab". Bob currently serves as Chairman of the Board of Directors for Kids' Chance of America, Inc. and was a founding board member and past president of Kids Chance of Florida, Inc.

Resources

For Further Reading, Research & Engagement

The topics covered in this book draw on decades of writing, advocacy, and hard-won industry experience. The following resources are offered for readers who want to dig deeper—whether you're an injured worker trying to understand the system, an employer looking to do better, a claims professional seeking best practices, a policymaker exploring reform, or simply someone who believes that a system built on the Great Compromise should actually deliver on its promise.

This is not an exhaustive bibliography. It is a curated starting point, organized by topic, designed to connect you with the people, organizations, and research that are shaping the future of workers' compensation—and, with any luck, its evolution into Workers' Recovery.

Research Organizations & Industry Data

These organizations produce the most credible, widely cited research on workers' compensation systems, costs, benefits, and outcomes. If you want to understand the data behind the debates, start here.

Workers' Compensation Research Institute (WCRI)

https://www.wcrinet.org

The gold standard for independent, evidence-based research on workers' compensation. WCRI produces state-by-state comparisons of claim costs, medical care patterns, return-to-work outcomes, and benefit adequacy.

Their CompScope studies are particularly valuable for understanding how different jurisdictions perform relative to one another. Essential reading for anyone serious about reform.

National Academy of Social Insurance (NASI)

https://www.nasi.org

NASI's annual report on Workers' Compensation: Benefits, Coverage, and Costs is one of the few publications that includes data on self-insurance and provides comprehensive estimates of premiums paid, indemnity and medical payments, and covered wages across all U.S. states and federal programs. Scholarly, thorough, and nonpartisan.

National Council on Compensation Insurance (NCCI)

https://www.ncci.com

NCCI is the primary source for actuarial data, rate-making, and statistical analysis in workers' compensation. Their Annual Statistical Bulletin provides a wide variety of data by state, including claims costs by injury type, loss development factors, premium level changes, and residual market information. Their Annual Issues Report provides excellent high-level analysis of industry trends.

International Association of Industrial Accident Boards and Commissions (IAIABC)

https://www.iaiabc.org

The IAIABC brings together government agencies, insurers, and researchers to improve workers' compensation administration. Their journal publishes peer-reviewed research on everything from interstate system comparisons to loss prevention to return-to-work best practices. A foundational resource for understanding the regulatory and administrative landscape.

Oregon Department of Consumer and Business Services — Premium Rate Ranking Study

https://www.oregon.gov/dcbs/reports/pages/index.aspx

The Oregon Premium Rate Ranking Study has become one of the most widely cited national benchmarks for comparing workers' compensation costs across states. Free to download and referenced by chambers of commerce, researchers, and policymakers nationwide.

Recovery, Return to Work & Disability Management

Workers' Recovery is fundamentally about better outcomes for injured workers. These resources provide the research foundation and practical frameworks for making recovery—not just claims closure—the goal.

National Institute of Disability Management and Research (NIDMAR)

https://www.nidmar.ca

NIDMAR has been a global leader in establishing professional standards for disability management and return-to-work practice. Their work with the International Social Security Association (ISSA) produced internationally recognized guidelines on good practice in return to work, endorsing a holistic, biopsychosocial approach that integrates prevention, workplace interventions, medical treatment, and vocational rehabilitation.

International Social Security Association (ISSA) — Return to Work Guidelines

https://www.issa.int

The ISSA Guidelines on Return to Work, developed in collaboration with NIDMAR, set out structures and mechanisms for effective RTW programs across 338 member organizations in 159 countries. They represent the global consensus on what good return-to-work practice looks like—comprehensive, integrated, and built around the biopsychosocial model.

Pacific Coast University for Workplace Health Sciences (PCU-WHS)

https://www.pcu-whs.ca

A degree-granting institution dedicated to creating and disseminating knowledge in workplace safety, health promotion, return to work, disability management, and comprehensive rehabilitation. Collaborates with Cornell University, Queensland University of Technology, and Bonn Rhein Sieg University. Offers distance learning programs for professionals in related fields.

The Biopsychosocial Model of Recovery

Much of the research supporting Workers' Recovery is grounded in the biopsychosocial model, which recognizes that recovery outcomes are influenced not just by the physical injury but by psychological factors (depression, catastrophizing, fear-avoidance) and social factors (workplace support, family dynamics, financial stress). Key researchers in this space include Dr. Robert Aurbach, whose work on optimizing outcomes in workers' compensation through behavioral and systemic interventions has been foundational to the Workers' Recovery framework.

Words Can Change Your Brain — Andrew Newberg, MD & Mark Robert Waldman

Referenced in the original "Case for Workers' Recovery" article series, this book explores the neurological impact of language on perception, behavior, and healing—directly relevant to how the words we use in workers' compensation (claimant vs. recovering worker, disability vs. impairment) shape outcomes.

The Human Cost: Mental Health, Chronic Pain & Opioids

Chapter 9 of this book addresses the human toll that system dysfunction inflicts on injured workers. These resources provide deeper context on the mental health, substance abuse, and social consequences of workplace injury.

Occupational Injury and Suicide Risk

Research in multiple countries has found that workers with occupational injuries face significantly elevated suicide risk compared to the general population. The combination of chronic pain, depression, financial distress, social isolation, and identity loss creates a risk profile that demands urgent attention. While the workers' compensation system does not track these outcomes, the research community is increasingly documenting them.

The Opioid Crisis and Workers' Compensation

The intersection of opioid dependency and workers' compensation is a critical area of ongoing research. Pioneering work by Dr. Gary M. Franklin at the Washington State Department of Labor and Industries revealed that nearly two percent of new workers' compensation claimants were already on opioids during the three months before their injuries. States including Washington and California have led in developing prescription drug monitoring programs and treatment guidelines.

Institute of Medicine – Substance Use Disorders in the U.S. Armed Forces (2012)

While focused on military populations, this study provides a rigorous framework for understanding how institutional systems can inadvertently contribute to substance use disorders—lessons directly applicable to the workers' compensation context.

Workers' Compensation Reform & Policy

The push for reform in workers' compensation is not new, but the arguments for it have never been stronger. These resources trace the history of reform efforts and frame the current landscape.

The 1972 National Commission on State Workmen's Compensation Laws

The landmark commission that produced a unanimous report with 84 recommendations for improving state workers' compensation programs. Its work established many of the benefit adequacy standards still referenced today. Understanding this commission's achievements—and why a similar effort would be nearly impossible in today's political environment—is essential context for any reform discussion.

RAND Institute for Civil Justice – Workers' Compensation Research

https://www.rand.org

RAND has produced significant wage-loss studies and evaluations of state workers' compensation systems, including an influential evaluation of California's permanent disability rating system. Their research methodology provides a model for evidence-based policy analysis in workers' compensation.

W.E. Upjohn Institute for Employment Research

https://www.upjohn.org

The Upjohn Institute has published important volumes on workplace injuries and diseases, benefit adequacy, and the intersection of workers' compensation with broader employment policy. Their work on the adequacy of earnings replacement in workers' compensation programs is particularly relevant to reform discussions.

U.S. Chamber of Commerce — Analysis of Workers' Compensation Laws

Published annually, this analysis tracks laws, benefits, and administrative features across all U.S. states, D.C., U.S. territories, and Canadian jurisdictions. A useful reference for understanding state-by-state variations in the system.

Association of Workers' Compensation Boards of Canada (AWCBC)

https://www.awcbc.org

Provides comprehensive, interactive public access to key statistical measures for Canadian workers' compensation systems, allowing data extraction and comparison across jurisdictions for injury, disease, and fatality statistics.

Workplace Safety & Loss Prevention

Prevention is the other side of the recovery coin. These resources address how workplaces can reduce injuries in the first place.

Occupational Safety and Health Administration (OSHA)

https://www.osha.gov

The federal agency responsible for workplace safety standards and enforcement. OSHA's resources include industry-specific guidelines, training materials, injury reporting requirements, and the Voluntary Protection Programs (VPP) that recognize workplaces with exemplary safety programs.

Safe Work Australia

https://www.safeworkaustralia.gov.au

Australia's national workplace safety and compensation body produces the Comparative Performance Monitoring report, which benchmarks jurisdictional performance across Australian and New Zealand workers' compensation systems—a useful model for how data-driven comparison can drive improvement.

Loss Prevention and Workers' Compensation Insurance

Workers' compensation insurers collect significant data through their loss prevention programs, but this information is underutilized for prevention purposes. Research in the IAIABC Journal has highlighted the need for more systematic, standardized approaches to hazard identification, safety program evaluation, and collaboration between insurers, employers, and regulatory agencies.

Technology, AI & the Future of Work

Chapter 12 of this book explores how emerging technologies are transforming both workplace risks and the administration of workers' compensation. The pace of change demands ongoing attention.

Artificial Intelligence in Claims Administration

AI and machine learning are increasingly being applied to claims triage, fraud detection, medical treatment review, and return-to-work prediction. While these tools hold genuine promise for reducing administrative burden and improving consistency, they also raise important questions about bias, transparency, and the role of human judgment in decisions that affect people's lives and livelihoods.

The Changing Workplace: Gig Economy, Remote Work & Emerging Risks

The traditional employment model that workers' compensation was built around is rapidly evolving. The growth of gig work, remote employment, and hybrid arrangements creates coverage gaps and jurisdictional questions that the existing system was not designed to address. Understanding these trends is essential for any meaningful reform effort.

Robotics, Automation & Workplace Safety

As discussed in Chapter 12, robotic systems, exoskeletons, and industrial automation are creating both new safety opportunities and new categories of workplace risk. Monitoring developments in this space through sources like the National Institute for Occupational Safety and Health (NIOSH) at https://www.cdc.gov/niosh/ is essential.

From the Author

The ideas in this book didn't emerge in isolation. They grew out of years of writing, teaching, and conversation with the workers' compensation community.

WorkCompCollege.com

https://www.workcompcollege.com

The author's primary educational platform, providing training, analysis, and commentary on workers' compensation issues for industry professionals at all levels.

Bob's Cluttered Desk (Blog)

https://www.bobsclutteredesk.com

The blog where much of the thinking behind this book was first developed—finding workers' compensation angles in the news, exploring industry absurdities with strategic humor, and making the case that a system built to serve injured workers should actually serve them.

WorkersRecovery.com

https://www.workersrecovery.com

The digital home for the Workers' Recovery concept and this book. Resources, updates, and opportunities to engage with the reform conversation.

"The Case for Workers' Recovery" — Article Series

Originally published in the IAIABC Journal with the support of Robert Aurbach, this article series gave structure and definition to the Workers' Recovery concept and served as the foundation for this book. It represents the moment when an ethereal idea gained a clearly defined body.

A Final Note: The most important resource in workers' compensation reform isn't a website, a study, or a publication. It's the willingness of the people within the system—claims professionals, employers, medical providers, regulators, and injured workers themselves—to demand better. The research tells us what's broken. The data shows us what works. The rest is up to us.

The system is not the purpose. The people are the purpose. They always were.

www.ingramcontent.com/pod-product-compliance
Lightning Source LLC
LaVergne TN
LVHW022040200926
848481LV00003B/722